Gardening in Containers

Created by the editorial staff of
ORTHO BOOKS

Designer
Gary Hespenheide

Ortho Books

Publisher
Robert B. Loperena

Editorial Director
Christine Jordan

Manufacturing Director
Ernie S. Tasaki

Managing Editor
Sally W. Smith

Editors
Robert J. Beckstrom
Michael D. Smith

Prepress Supervisor
Linda M. Bouchard

Sales & Marketing Manager
David C. Jose

Graphics Coordinator
Sally J. French

Publisher's Assistant
Joni Christiansen

Address all inquiries to
Ortho Books
Box 5006
San Ramon, CA 94583-0906

© 1984, 1996 Monsanto Company
All rights reserved

1 2 3 4 5 6 7 8 9
96 97 98 99 2000 01

ISBN 0-89721-282-7
Library of Congress Catalog Card Number 95-68611

THE SOLARIS GROUP
2527 Camino Ramon
San Ramon, CA 94583-0906

Acknowledgments

Editor
Larry Hodgson

Consultant
Barbara Ferguson Stremple

Editorial Coordinator
Cass Dempsey

Copyeditor
Judith Dunham

Proofreaders
Alicia K. Eckley
Kate St. Clair

Indexer
Elinor Lindheimer

Illustrator
Deborah Cowder

Color Separations by
Color Tech Corp.

Printed in the USA by
Banta Book Group

Designers
Names of designers are followed by the page numbers on which their work appears. R = right, C = center, L = left, T = top, B = bottom.

Bob Clark: 37B
Bill Hollborn: 21R, 40, 43
Ellen Pearce: 1

Special Thanks to
Kathy Barry & Bob Burnett
City College of San Francisco
Mr. & Mrs. Charles Davis
Chip Kenney
Ellen McKaskle
Sloat Garden Center
Katharine & Dan Whalen

Photographers
Names of photographers are followed by the page numbers on which their work appears. R = right, C = center, L = left, T = top, B = bottom.

William C. Aplin: 56
Cathy Wilkinson Barash: PHOTO/NATS: 81R, 87L
Laurie Black: 25, 32TL, 32TR, 32CL, 32CR, 49T
John Blaustein: 11TL, 11TR, 41
Margarite Bradley/Positive Images: 72R
Patricia J. Bruno/Positive Images: 83R
Gay Bumgarner: 7
Gay Bumgarner: PHOTO/NATS: 63L
Karen Bussolini/Positive Images: 85L
Priscilla Connell: PHOTO/NATS: 65R
Crandall & Crandall: 55L, 68R, 87R
R. Todd Davis Photography: 30
Christine M. Douglas: 6B, 12B, 21L, 27L, 75R
Mary Ann Evans: 54, 66R, 90L
Derek Fell: Front cover, 3T, 3CT, 3CB, 4-5, 29, 34-35, 38T, 38B, 44-45, 47T, 55R, 59, 62R, 66L, 68L, 69L, 69R, 76R, 79R, 82L, 82R, 84R, 88R, 89L, 89R, 90R, back cover TR & BL
David Goldberg: 1, 9, 15T, 15B, 18, 19T, 19C, 19B, 21R, 22T, 22B, 27R, 37B, 40, 43, 49B, 52, back cover TL
Jennifer Graylock: PHOTO/NATS: 64L, 80L
Harry Haralambou/Positive Images: 74R, 88L
Jerry Howard/Positive Images: 6T, 28, 46, 65L, 70R, 71L, 79L, 84L, 86L, 91R, back cover BR
Michael Landis: 8, 11B, 12TL, 12TR
P. Lindtner: 76L
Robert E. Lyons: PHOTO/NATS: 67L, 77L, 77R
Ivan Massar/Positive Images: 62L
Michael McKinley: 32B, 86R
Jack Napton: 72L
Ortho Photo Library: 3B, 47B, 53, 57, 60-61, 75L, 78L, 80R, 81L, 83L, 85R
Jerry Pavia: 36, 37T, 58, 64R, 67R, 73R
Pam Peirce: 78R
Ann Reilly: PHOTO/NATS: 63R
Paul Rezendes/Positive Images: 70L
Pam Spaulding/Positive Images: 71R
Mark Turner: 23
Lee Anne White/Positive Images: 73L, 74L, 91L

Front Cover
From the cast-off shoes to the oak barrel, this charming garden is almost entirely composed of containers—proving that only imagination limits what can be done with a limited space.

Title Page
Flowers and ivy-filled pots enliven steps to a patio.

Back Cover
Top left: Planting containers is easy to do. It requires few tools and even less time to make plants comfortable in their new homes.

Top right: Container planting allows a garden to bloom on a raised deck.

Bottom left: An unusual gourd shows this primrose off to perfection.

Bottom right: By planting in containers, everyone can have home-grown vegetables from limited space.

Gardening in Containers

Gardening in Containers

With container gardening, an outdoor area filled with living greenery and perfumed flowers is no longer restricted to landed homeowners: Everyone, everywhere, even urban apartment and condominium dwellers, can have a green space to call their own.

Container gardening gives gardeners the ultimate in flexibility. You can create a mini-landscape that includes virtually every element of a planted yard. You can take advantage of whatever space is available, from a vast terrace to a narrow window ledge. You can grow a limitless range of plants—flowers, fruits, vegetables, vines, shrubs, and even trees—using just about anything that can hold soil: boxes, bowls, tubs, clay pots, ceramic pots, hanging baskets, wire mesh.

This book will help you enjoy all the opportunities offered by container gardening to create an outdoor living space. It is full of information on how to select plants, when and how to plant them, and how to care for them. It discusses how to build, buy, and maintain containers in and around apartments, townhouses, roof gardens, balconies, decks, and patios. This is a book not only for the dedicated gardener, but also for the many people who may not pursue gardening as a hobby but who do enjoy the ambience and color that plants bring to a home's surroundings.

Strategically placed potted plants complete a flowering display. When the blooms fade, the small pots will be replaced and large pots replanted, so the garden never has an off-season.

THE ADVANTAGES OF CONTAINER GARDENS

Far from restricting your gardening options, container gardening extends them. Consider the flexibility of this kind of gardening and its suitability to limited gardening space, lack of time for gardening, frequent moves, and other aspects of modern lifestyles. You can develop a beautiful container garden in a spot where poor soil—or even no soil at all—would make landscaping nearly impossible. You can make much more use of frost-tender plants because you can move them indoors or into a protected part of the garden on cool nights. Container plants heat up more rapidly in the spring, giving you a head start on spring color, and likewise cool off more quickly in the autumn, filling your growing space with colorful fall shades weeks ahead of in-ground gardens. Container gardens have a very special, focused beauty of their own, and are not merely containerized replicas of traditional gardens.

Mobility

One advantage of container plants is that you can move them—and that they can move with you. Today's lifestyles call for maximum flexibility, a willingness to adapt to change, and the

Top: Flowering indoors during the winter, clivia (see page 78) will return to the outdoor garden with warmer weather. Bottom: A conventional garden is not a possibility for this apartment dweller, but ingenuity prevails: plants rest on a decorative balcony, fill planters hung from its railing and from the fire escape above, and even cling to the building's wall.

capacity to move at a moment's notice. Where a mere generation ago people commonly set up house and expected to stay put for the rest of their lives, people today see nothing in regularly changing apartments or homes, or moving from city to city or state to state. Under such circumstances, it's hard to put down roots and even more difficult to create an outdoor living space, unless you garden in containers.

Traditional gardens are basically permanent. With their roots firmly anchored in the soil, most garden plants are unwilling to follow their owners during a move, and are not even very gracious about being moved from one part of the same garden to another. They resent having their roots pruned heavily and may die back if the procedure isn't carried out when they are dormant, usually in fall or winter. An heirloom plant—perhaps a seedling taken from a childhood home or a tree planted by your child—may simply have to be left behind, that is, if you planted it in the ground.

Plants in containers can be moved as easily as furniture, however. With a few precautions (see right) you can bundle up your garden and take it with you to your new home.

Containers also allow plants to be moved indoors whenever necessary. This could simply

Moving With Plants

Plants in the ground stay behind when you move to another home. This is certainly not the case with container plants: you can carefully pack and move plants in containers at a moment's notice, even if they are in full growth and bloom. You can then reassemble the entire container garden upon arrival—or whenever you are ready, as container-grown plants easily put up with less-than-ideal conditions for a few days while you tend to more urgent matters. Recently dug garden plants, on the other hand, stressed from a long journey, may require that you plant the garden before you have unpacked the furniture.

Moving container plants within the same city or state is not difficult. Just let them dry out for a few days beforehand, though not to the point of wilting. They'll be lighter, the pots won't be damp and slippery, and there'll be no moisture to soak through the packing material. Set the pots carefully into cardboard boxes, and stabilize them by stuffing newspaper into any open spaces. Protect them from frost or extreme heat by covering them in multiple layers of newspaper. For safe moving of hanging plants, take them down, pull the foliage above each plant, and roll it, pot and all, in newspaper, forming a cone that you can then secure with tape. If the move will take more than a few hours and the temperature is extreme, you might consider using a separate vehicle that can be heated or air-conditioned. If you move the plants yourself and have to stop the car for any length of time, make sure you park out of the hot sun.

Before moving plants between states, always verify current regulations concerning plant imports. California, for example, has stringent rules about importing plants, whereas other states do not have restrictions on this kind of move. Import regulations make moving plants to and from foreign countries a very difficult task, but it may nevertheless be possible if you do the proper paperwork beforehand.

If establishing and maintaining a full-fledged permanent garden is not realistic for you, you can still know the pleasure of growing things. Just fill a few containers with your favorite flowers and cluster them where you'll be able to enjoy them every day.

be to create a temporary display—a technique long used by the Japanese, who traditionally bring a particularly attractive bonsai indoors when a visitor is expected—or to protect tender plants from the elements (see Winter Protection on page 25). Gardeners who live in a cold climate can create an entire indoor/outdoor garden by moving tender plants outdoors in the spring and back inside for the winter.

Versatility

A special advantage of containers is that they enable you to enjoy plants where a "dirt garden" would not be feasible—on pavement, a rooftop, a balcony, an outside stairway, or a fire escape. Because they don't have to be anchored in the ground, container gardens flourish wherever adequate light and access for watering and fertilizing make them possible.

If you have only a 10th-floor balcony or a postage-stamp concrete courtyard, bring it to life with container plants. There is no reason why you shouldn't look out onto lush shrubs and trees and bright flowers, or why you can't enjoy homegrown fruit and vegetables, as long as your garden spot receives enough light. The only limitation to container gardening high above the ground is weight—bear in mind that a newly watered container, particularly a big one holding a tree, is very heavy.

Potted plants of every sort bring a lush beauty to a small townhouse courtyard.

Focal Points

Setting a stage for container plants enhances the beauty of each plant. Its beauty is also brought out by the very fact that it is in a container. When you put a plant in a box, tub, or

The Vertical Garden

If your garden is too small to accommodate all the plants you want to grow, try using the vertical dimension. Every smooth vertical surface is a potential gardening area.

Although some experts advise against planting vine crops such as melons, cucumbers, and squashes in a small garden, the gardener working in a small space can assume that any wide-spreading vine can easily be trained to grow up instead of out. A vertical vine can't support heavy fruits such as melons and squash, but a sling made of an old pair of panty hose will take the weight off the vines. For training plants upward, you can use a trellis, string, or plastic mesh. Garden centers sell clips specially designed for holding vines to wood supports.

You can also display planter boxes of various dimensions on a fence or wall, supported by brackets or shelves. Just be sure to allow for the full, filled weight of the planter when you install the supports.

pot, you immediately give it new character. It becomes an individual shrub with its own distinctiveness. It is spotlighted.

Simply going to the nursery and looking at the most common plants with an eye to placing them in containers can change your whole idea of how to use them. Plants seem to have both a garden personality and a container personality. For example, when a low-growing juniper is hugging the ground, it's a ground cover—but when it is elevated in a box, pinched and pruned for a windswept look, it becomes a work of art.

Keeping the Best Plant Forward

Traditional gardens have periods of extreme beauty—perhaps when bulbs are in bloom in the spring, then later when roses are in full flower, then again when foliage changes color in the fall—but are rarely at their best the year around. This need not be the case with container gardens. As potted plants come into bloom, highlight them by placing the containers in full view. As they fade, whisk them out of sight to a spot where they can recuperate while other plants take their place.

At the same time, you can be growing a pot of annuals to their full color and glory, or waiting for a pot of bulbs to blossom in an out-of-the-way corner where the plants are easy to care for but are out of sight until they reach their peak.

CONTAINER CULTURE

Growing plants in containers exposes them to conditions quite unlike those experienced by plants grown in the ground. It is only normal, then, that their soil, water, fertilizer, and cultural requirements will also differ. Understanding these requirements makes it easier to meet them, assuring you of a container garden that gives you constant satisfaction.

Soil Mixes

Soil mixes used for container gardening are not the same as those used for traditional gardens. Garden plants often grow in rather heavy soils with lots of clay, but do well when earthworms and other soil organisms are hard at work loosening the soil on a regular basis. Trees and large shrubs actually need heavy soils to support their weight. In pots, though, where earthworms are absent, heavy soils become too compact, cutting off essential supplies of oxygen to the roots of the plants. The heaviness of garden soil is also a disadvantage in a pot, because containers need to be as light as possible so they can be moved easily.

For these reasons, container-grown plants need a special soil mix, one that is lightweight

Red-and-yellow gaillardia enlivens an arrangement of potted plants while it is in bloom. When its flowers wane, it will be retired to an unobtrusive spot.

and well drained. Garden stores and nurseries sell these "houseplant" or "potted plant" mixtures, or even "hanging basket" mixes, under a wide variety of trade names, but all have the same light, fluffy texture that is essential for container culture.

Some container soils are labeled "soilless mixes" or "synthetic soils," but they aren't artificial. In fact, most contain natural ingredients only. The ingredients may vary, but the principle behind all mixes is the same. Soil for container gardening must provide three elements.

•Fast drainage of water through the soil

•Air in the soil after drainage

•A reservoir of water remaining in the soil after drainage

Most important in any container mix is the air left in the soil after drainage. Plant roots require air for growth and respiration. A heavy garden soil has little pore space between soil particles. When water is applied to the soil, it drives out air by filling the small pore spaces.

A container mix has both small and large pores (micropores and macropores). When the mix is irrigated, water is held in the micropores but quickly drains through the macropores, allowing air to follow.

Most container mixes are composed of an organic component and a mineral component. The organic part of the mix, which varies from region to region, may be peat moss, redwood sawdust, wood shavings, hardwood bark, fir bark, pine bark, or any combination.

The mineral part may be vermiculite, perlite (sponge rock), pumice, builder's sand, granite sand, rock wool, or a combination of any two or three. The most commonly used minerals are vermiculite, perlite, and sand.

Vermiculite is made up of an expanded mineral, mica. Under heat treatment, the mineral flakes expand with air spaces to 20 times their original thickness. Each vermiculite granule absorbs water and minerals like a tiny sponge and releases them slowly as needed.

Perlite starts off as a granitelike volcanic material. Like vermiculite, it is crushed and heated (to 1,500° to 2,000° F), causing it to expand like popcorn. Unlike vermiculite, however, perlite particles are sealed and do not retain water, so perlite dries out faster than vermiculite. Its main advantage, besides its light weight, is that it leaves plentiful spaces where air can circulate freely and through

which water can drain readily. Sand and perlite are often used interchangeably, depending on how heavy a mix is desired.

Sand is commonly used as a component of container soil mixes, and also for rooting cuttings. It helps ensure aeration while maintaining good drainage. It is very helpful when you need a bit of extra weight—to keep tall plants from being knocked over on a windswept balcony, for example.

Not all sands are useful in containers. Beach sand and road sand often contain salt and can kill plants when used in potting mixes. For gardening, washed and screened quartz sand is best. Unscreened sand contains a range of particle sizes and does not aerate as well. Coarse sand is preferred because of its aerating qualities.

Plants vary greatly in their requirements for aeration, the air space in the soil after water has drained away. For example, azaleas and some ferns have very high aeration requirements. Commercial growers often grow them in straight coarse peat moss to get this high aeration. Begonias, gardenias, podocarpus, rhododendrons, snapdragons, and most foliage plants require high aeration. Camellias, chrysanthemums, and poinsettias are intermediate in their aeration requirements. Carnations, geraniums, ivies, and most conifers tolerate poor aeration.

Aeration is closely related to drainage. As water drains from the mix, air replaces it, so mixes that drain well are also well aerated.

Water moves by continuous capillary action through soil in the same way that it moves through a blotter. Porous material such as gravel or large air spaces will break that continuity, and water will build up wherever the continuity is broken. Water collects and builds up at the drain holes of a pot. The bottom inch or two of soil is soggy after a watering, but the soil above is drier, the water having been pulled out by the force of gravity. Because of this effect, deep containers drain better than shallow ones, even when both are filled with the same type of soil.

You can observe this most easily with a sponge. Hold a sponge flat under a tap and soak it with water. If you let it rest flat on your hand, it will stop dripping in a moment. If the sponge is 2 inches thick, it acts like potting mix in a 2-inch-deep container. Next hold the sponge by one edge and let it hang sideways. More water will drip from it. Additional air has entered the upper edge, "aerating" it more thoroughly. Wait until it stops dripping, then turn the sponge, this time so the end you just held hangs downward. Again, more water will spill from it. The thicker the sponge, the more water is pulled from it by gravity, and the more air enters it. Potting mixes release water in exactly the same way, depending on the depth of the container.

Selecting a mix Container mixes come in two general grades. One is made for small pots and indoor use, and contains a large amount of peat moss. This mix is usually called "potting mix." The other is sand-based, with composted sawdust or ground bark added. It is usually called a "planting mix," and is most suitable for deeper containers. Both mixes are usually adequate for the purpose for which they are made.

Many have been pasteurized and are free of weed seeds, insects, and pathogens.

This doesn't mean that you shouldn't alter the mix you buy. On the contrary—if the mix is so lightweight that the container will tip over in a slight wind, by all means add sand. Some gardeners, unwilling to leave well enough alone, add garden topsoil to the mix when planting in containers. But when you add soil, you lose all the advantages of a sterilized mix. For example, if you are growing container tomatoes in a soilless mix to avoid soilborne tomato diseases, adding garden soil would invite the same diseases you are trying to prevent.

Pasteurized soilless mixes are free of disease organisms, weed seeds, and insects. Many already include all the nutrients needed for initial plant growth. Soilless mixes are ready for immediate use. A 2-cubic-foot bag supplies enough "soil" for 20 to 22 gallon-sized containers or for 35 to 40 pots that are 6 inches deep.

Common mineral components for container soil mix are vermiculite (top left), perlite (top right), and sand (bottom).

Top: Soil mix for containers includes an organic material, which may be peat moss (left) or fir bark (right). Bottom: If you plan to install large planters such as these on a rooftop, you can reduce the weight considerably by using a soil mix formulated for containers, rather than dirt direct from the ground.

You'll need 4 cubic feet for a planter box 24 inches by 36 inches by 8 inches deep.

The light weight of peat moss and vermiculite mixes comes in handy when you need to move containers from one spot to another, or when you create a garden on a roof or balcony, where weight can be a problem. Mixes containing perlite and organic matter often weigh less than half as much as garden soil when both are soaked.

Planting and Transplanting

It's best to wet a lightweight synthetic mix before using it—a pot filled with dry mix is difficult to wet properly. The easiest and least messy way is to add water directly to the plastic bags containing the mix. Hold the top of each bag and knead the water into the mixture until it is evenly moist. Let the entire bag sit overnight before using to ensure an even distribution of moisture throughout the mixture. If

When You Bring a Plant Home

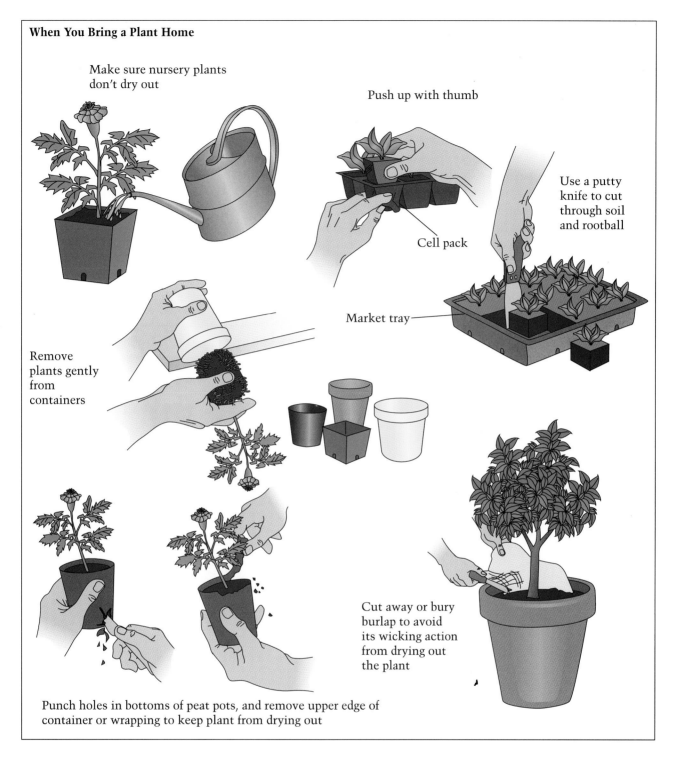

Make sure nursery plants don't dry out

Push up with thumb

Cell pack

Use a putty knife to cut through soil and rootball

Market tray

Remove plants gently from containers

Cut away or bury burlap to avoid its wicking action from drying out the plant

Punch holes in bottoms of peat pots, and remove upper edge of container or wrapping to keep plant from drying out

you don't plan to use all the mix immediately, keep it moist by tying the top of the bag tightly.

In the past, gardeners were frequently advised to add a "drainage layer"—an inch of gravel—to the bottom of the pot. Modern research has shown that this can actually impede drainage by disrupting the downward flow of water. Instead, fill the bottom of the container with premoistened soil mix to the depth of the rootball of the plant.

Planting in a container is a simple task: Just set the plant into the container soil at the level at which it grew in the nursery. Then fill the container, firming the mix down, especially near the edges. After placing the plant in the container, water the soil thoroughly. The soil, when settled, should be ½ to 1 inch below the rim of the container to allow *one* application of water to moisten the rootball and drain through the container. If the watering space is too shallow, you may have to water, let it drain into the soil, and then water again.

Pay special attention to watering during the first few weeks after transplanting. It is important to keep the rootball moist until the roots have spread into the surrounding soil, because soil differences may make the rootball dry out even though the surrounding soil is wet.

When you pick up plants at the nursery, chances are that they will continue to perform well if you care for them properly. Mishandling of plants most often occurs during the first few days of ownership. Here are some tips on how to handle fresh-from-the-nursery plants.

If you run out of time to plant all your purchases and must hold some plants, make sure that they don't dry out in the interim. Water

them as you would any container plant until you are ready to remove them from the nursery containers. A damp (not wet) rootball will not shatter or stick to the edge of the container.

Nursery plants are generally grown in plastic, fiber, or metal containers (see page 13). Remove the plants from cell packs the easy way: squeeze the bottom of the container in the cell pack to force the rootball above the lip. When removing plants from market trays, cut the soil in blocks. Use a putty knife for cutting the soil and removing the rootball. Don't pull plants out of containers or you'll damage the roots.

Ask the nursery to cut straight-sided cans because they are otherwise hard to remove from the plants. Plants grown in cans, pots, or tubs with sloping sides can be tapped out of

When You Plant

Plant at proper soil level

Too high

Too low

Just right

Prune roots of pot-bound plants

Bark chunks or pebbles

Ground cover planting

their containers. Hold the container upside down and tap it against a ledge. Hold the rootball by placing the stem or trunk of the plant between your fingers or hands.

Handle biodegradable containers carefully. Small plants may come in peat pots, compressed peat pellets, or paper pots; larger shrubs may come in fiber pots or may be balled and burlapped (B&B). Plant peat pots and pellets below the soil line. With peat pots, punch holes in the bottoms and cut off the exposed upper edges of the containers. The rootball dries out quickly if any part of a peat pot or wrapping remains above the soil surface.

Fiber pots, often used for shrubs and small trees, will disintegrate over time but for container use are best removed as with any other pot. Burlap can be removed entirely if this is feasible; if not, leave it on the rootball, but cut off the top flaps to below soil level. Any burlap remaining should be completely buried; exposed sections promote rapid evaporation, which causes the rootball to dry out.

Plants grown in pots often form long roots outside the rootball that run along the sides and bottom of the container. Don't hesitate to prune them before setting the plant into a larger container. Just make three or four cuts from top to bottom with a sharp knife down the side of the rootball. This pruning will speed up the formation of new roots and the penetration of roots into the soil surrounding the rootball.

You can keep container gardens going for several years in the same soil, but most soil mixes, unless they are renewed occasionally, slowly become compact and waterlogged, stifling plant growth and sometimes leading to root rot. In most cases, keeping the soil mix in good shape is as simple as renewing the top 3 to 4 inches annually. Remove the top layer of old mix (add it to the compost bin) and replace it with an equal amount of fresh soil, mixing it in with the layers below. For containers to be planted with annuals and vegetables, renew the soil in the spring before planting.

For perennials, the best time to renew the soil is when they have grown to the point where they need division, about once every two to three years. As you remove and separate them, change part of the soil mix as well.

For permanent plantings such as shrubs and trees, you can renew the soil each spring by carefully removing the top few inches of

mix. The bottom layers of soil, filled with roots, are difficult to renew. This is why it is best to use a mix designed for woody plants, one that is rich in sand and with few compressible products such as vermiculite. Even mixes designed for trees and shrubs can eventually become so

Top: Transplanting is simple. Place the plant into the new pot at the same level at which it was growing in the nursery container, fill the pot with soil mix, and press it firmly so the plant is stable. Bottom: It is important to periodically renew the soil of a plant that remains in the same container for a number of years. Here, after the top few inches of old soil have been removed, fresh soil is added to the pot.

compacted that drainage is severely reduced. When plants show signs of severe stress—slow growth, small leaves, reduced flowering—remove them when they are dormant and replace the mix entirely. This shouldn't be necessary, at least under normal growing conditions, more than once every seven or eight years. When repotting shrubs and trees, don't hesitate to prune back any dead or dying roots as well as those circling the container. Trees and shrubs repotted into fresh mix will soon grow as vigorously as ever.

The use of a lightweight soil mix—peat moss and perlite or vermiculite—lessens the weight problem, but a moist mix still weighs far more than a dry one. Before moving a heavy container, then, it pays to wait until the soil is nearly dry.

For moving large, heavy tubs, a dolly on casters is a welcome aid. In fact, it pays to attach a set of casters permanently to the base of any large box or tub.

Casters make a container easier to move, and they also create air space beneath the container, robbing earwigs and slugs of a potential hiding place.

If you have many containers, you will find a hand truck to be a useful gadget. Attaching a trash bag to the hand truck lightens the chore of garden cleanup.

Watering

Perhaps the key factor to success in container gardening is proper watering. Plants growing in the ground often send roots out deep into the soil below them or long distances from the main stalk and are therefore able to seek out water even when the soil near their bases is nearly dry. Plants grown in containers don't have this advantage: they are entirely dependent on the water available to them within the confines of their pots. When that is gone, they begin to wilt, indicating that root damage is already taking place. Most plants recover well from slight wiltings—some, such as impatiens, coleus, strawberries, and tomatoes, can seem to collapse entirely, but make an equally dramatic and speedy recovery when watered promptly. Yet all plants eventually die if their watering needs are not met.

How frequently you should water depends on many factors: soil mix, presence or absence of mulches, type and size of container, temperature, wind, sunlight, natural rainfall, humidity, and type of plant grown.

The types of soil recommended under Soil Mixes on page 9 all have excellent water-retention capacities. One reason that ordinary garden soil is not recommended for use in containers is that, when confined to a pot, it is unable to hold enough water to maintain healthy growth. If your area is subject to frequent droughts, consider increasing the proportions of water-retentive agents, such as vermiculite and peat moss, in the mixes you use and decreasing the products that stimulate fast drainage, such as sand and perlite.

The type and size of container help to maintain an acceptable water level. A plant in a porous clay pot, for example, needs water more frequently than one in a plastic or glazed pot. Some gardeners solve the evaporation problem by placing the pot inside a larger pot and insulating the space between the two with peat moss or perlite and layers of charcoal and/or gravel. If you do this, be careful to use an outer pot with a drainage hole, or the insulation will become soaked during heavy rains.

Large pots hold more soil—and therefore more moisture-retentive soil mix—than do smaller pots. Therefore, it is often best to use the largest containers you can easily handle, rather than small pots, which will require frequent watering. One way to solve the evaporation problem with small pots is to group them together in a wood box. A 14-inch by 24-inch box that is 10 inches deep will hold two 5-gallon containers or a group of 6-inch pots. Put ground bark or peat moss around the pots for insulation and as a mulch.

If watering according to the calendar is impossible, when do you water? Experienced gardeners often develop ways to judge watering needs, such as lifting containers to determine their weight (dry soil is lighter than damp soil), studying soil appearance (moist soil is darker than damp soil), and assessing appearance of the plants (a slight graying of the foliage can indicate a need for watering long before the plant actually wilts). For most people, though, touching the mix is the best way. Sink an index finger into the mix to the second joint. If the soil feels dry, it's time to water. If not, you can wait and then test again.

One of the great values of synthetic soil mixes compared with garden soils is that they won't become waterlogged as long as the container drains properly. This means that, if necessary, you can water when most convenient to your schedule, not just when the mix is nearing dryness. If you are going to be away but the soil in the containers is still slightly moist, for example, simply give them a thorough watering before you go. You can also water thoroughly in the morning of a hot summer day, in anticipation of a late-afternoon drought.

There is a fine line between a container that holds moisture well and one that can become waterlogged. Although watering is a major preoccupation for container gardeners, it is just as important to ensure that excess moisture drains away. Soil sours, roots rot, and root-killing mineral salts build up in any container that drains poorly.

Ideally, only containers supplied with drainage holes should be used for container gardening. Many pots already have one or more drainage holes in the bottom; others have a plug that can be removed for outdoor use. When holes are not present, they can be drilled. One ¼-inch drainage hole per square foot of surface is usually sufficient to ensure

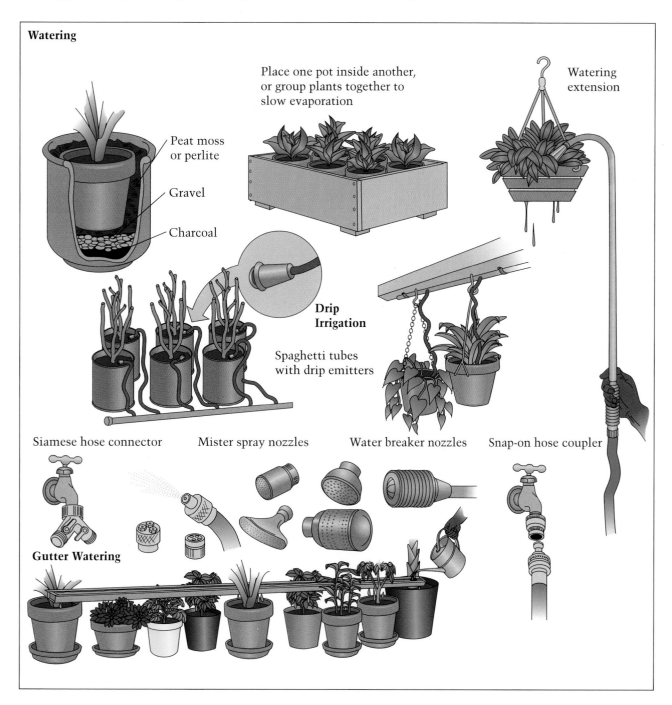

Watering

Place one pot inside another, or group plants together to slow evaporation

Watering extension

Peat moss or perlite

Gravel

Charcoal

Drip Irrigation

Spaghetti tubes with drip emitters

Siamese hose connector   Mister spray nozzles   Water breaker nozzles   Snap-on hose coupler

Gutter Watering

To remove excess water from under a heavy container, use a turkey baster. Keep the baster for garden use—do not return it to the kitchen.

good drainage. If a container drains slowly, more or larger drainage holes, or a faster-draining mix, or both are needed.

Containers without drainage holes are not good choices for outdoor use. Inevitably, a heavy rain or overwatering causes the soil they hold to become waterlogged, resulting in sick or dying plants. If for any reason the container that meets your needs lacks a capacity for natural drainage, you can tip it on its side or use a turkey baster to remove some of the excess water. For containerized water gardens (see page 29), however, containers without drainage holes, or whose drainage holes can be plugged, are ideal.

If a container is set in a saucer, empty the saucer after every watering. If the container is too heavy to lift, empty the saucer with a turkey baster. Unless you can empty the at-

tached saucer of a hanging planter after every watering, remove the saucer permanently.

Water-absorbent polymers   The capacity of potting mix to hold water can be improved by the addition of water-absorbent polymers, which can absorb and hold hundreds of times their own weight in water. When purchased, polymers—also called hydrogels or polyacrylamides—look like simple white crystals. When water is added to them, they act like sponges, swelling up to many times their original size, growing to look like chunks of clear jelly. Their purpose, when mixed with potting soil, is to hold water and release it slowly as plants need it, thus reducing watering. They are biodegradable products but can be expected to last at least five years under normal use.

Studies of these products often show contradictory results—obviously their efficiency varies according to local conditions—but many experts agree that they are very useful in containers. Although claims are made that water-absorbent polymers can reduce watering frequency to once every two to three weeks, this is unlikely in containers outdoors. But you can expect them to reduce watering frequencies somewhat, depending on the water-holding capacity of the soil to begin with. If that capacity was good, the polymers will make little difference. But if the capacity was low, you may see a considerable improvement.

Don't expect polymers to conserve water: if they reduce watering frequencies by about one-half, they need twice as much water to regain their form. For maximum efficiency, apply water slowly to allow them to absorb as much as possible.

Water-absorbent polymers are least efficient in small pots (less than 8 inches in diameter) and in cool, humid climates. In fact, they may not make a noticeable difference in watering frequency under such circumstances. They may, however, be lifesavers in locations where conditions are hot and dry.

Expect other benefits from polymers. They tend to buffer soil temperatures, keeping the soil cool on hot days and protecting the soil to a certain extent from frost. They can also absorb liquid fertilizers and release them bit by bit over a longer period than do regular soil mixes.

Application rates for water-absorbent polymers vary from product to product. It is best to follow manufacturers' instructions, although a rate of 4 pounds of polymers per cubic yard of mix is generally acceptable. If possible, mix them into the soil before planting, as they are difficult to apply evenly to containers once plants have been added. Some soil mixes already contain polymers; check the labels before adding more.

Always experiment with polymers before using them on a large scale. They can be very efficient under some conditions, but are almost ineffective under others.

Hand watering For most people, especially those with small container gardens, hand watering is the most obvious way to supply plants with moisture when nature is uncooperative.

With many container gardens—especially those located far from an outdoor faucet, such as most balcony and rooftop gardens—carrying water from the kitchen or bathroom is the easiest approach. For small numbers of containers, pitchers, pails, drinking glasses, or other household vessels may be the only "watering devices" you will ever need. If you have many plants, you will find a watering can more efficient, less messy, and far less time-consuming. A 1- to 2-gallon can is inexpensive, fits into a normal sink, and holds a fairly large quantity of water, reducing the number of trips to and from the water source. Watering cans with removable nozzles are particularly useful, as they break up the force of the flow, allowing you to water

Water-absorbing polymers can be mixed with the soil in a container. The dry crystals (top) take up a great volume of water, expanding to many times their original size (center), then slowly release the moisture to the plant.
Bottom: For many container gardens, a watering can is a satisfactory method of watering. Use a removable nozzle (on the windowsill) for seedlings.

seedlings and young plants without knocking them over.

If you have several plants and access to a water hookup of any kind, hoses are a better choice than watering cans, if only because you won't find yourself running to and from the indoor faucet so often. Just add an adjustable sprayer with an on-off button to one end of the hose, attach the other to the faucet, turn it on—and you're in business. Buy a weather- and kink-resistant hose of an appropriate length for your needs. These hoses are generally sold in 25-foot, 50-foot, and 100-foot lengths. As even 25 feet can be too much for a small container garden, on a balcony, for example—and who wants extra hose lying where it can trip you or visitors?—you can easily cut a hose to the length you need and refit it with a new adapter.

If you do not have an outdoor faucet, consider running a hose from the kitchen or bathroom sink and out through a window or door. By using a Siamese hose connector with double shutoff valves at the faucet end, you'll be able to leave the hose connected and functioning throughout the growing season, yet not lose the use of the faucet.

For watering hanging baskets set beyond your reach, consider adding a watering extension to your hose or buying a squeeze bottle specifically designed for this purpose. You can also add misters to a hose.

Drip irrigation   The ultimate in watering ease is a drip irrigation system, which leads water directly to the plants you grow. Just turn it on and let it water your containers for you. Water is applied drop by drop with little water loss, helping to conserve water. A drip system also facilitates gardening in sites that do not receive water from rainfall, such as under an overhanging roof.

A drip irrigation system consists of a length of standard-size hose that branches off into smaller individual hoses, each of which applies water directly to a specific pot. A typical system includes a main line to the container-garden area, a manifold separating the flow of water to two or more secondary or branch lines, and tube-end closures for each of these lines so that water is forced into the individual watering devices (drippers, sprinklers, or sprayers). Connectors, elbows (for sharp bends), and tees (to connect two lines to one) link the system together. Small tee connectors are added to the branch lines, one for each spot to be watered, and thin "spaghetti" tubing then leads to the individual watering devices. Make sure you install a filter and a water pressure regulator between the faucet and the main line. Many municipalities require an antisyphon (a valve that prevents contaminated water from flowing back into the domestic water supply).

Drippers are the most popular watering devices attached to container-garden irrigation systems. Some kinds include on-line water pressure regulators, which eliminate the need for a pressure regulator at the main water source. Sprayers are popular in dusty conditions as they help keep the foliage clean, but they lose considerably more water to evaporation than drippers and wet a deck or patio as well as the containers. They usually can be adjusted to water in full, half, or quarter circles. Mister spray nozzles, especially popular in arid climates, gives container plants the fog they need on hot, dry days. They should be on a separate system from drippers or sprayers, as they are not used at the same time.

Drip Irrigation Parts

Timer

Pressure gauge

Emitter

Antisiphon valve

Pressure regulator

Filter

Left: Drip tubing leads from water line to container.
Right: With well-developed foliage to hide behind and a raised deck to cover the main lines, an irrigation system can be almost invisible.

Various manufacturers use different calibers of lines and tubing. Therefore, it is best to stick with products from one company or at least to check for compatibility before extending your system. Check, too, for the maximum number of watering devices that can be connected to the system. This number varies considerably according to tubing diameter.

Generally speaking, one or two drippers per container, depending on its size, are sufficient, although deep planters and long flower boxes may require three or more, set at about 12-inch intervals. Only one mister is needed per container.

Depending on conditions, drip irrigation should be left on for an hour or two, the time needed to moisten the mix entirely. When water begins to run out of the drainage holes, turn off the system. After a few weeks of testing, you'll have a fairly good idea about just how long your drip system should be left in operation.

Drip irrigation is efficient and easy to use, but without proper planning is highly visible. Try running lines along the periphery of the growing space and behind the pots, even if this means using an extra length of hose. Individual spaghetti tubing can then be led up the back of the pots before being clamped into place. Once plants begin to grow, the drip irrigation will be quite unobtrusive.

Watering hanging baskets requires a bit more care. Run lines up the side of the supporting structure in the least obtrusive spot, then across the top. Spaghetti tubing can then drop down to individual drippers at the point of attachment of the hanging basket.

Subirrigation systems are a type of drip system that allows the watering devices to be hidden out of sight in the soil, the most effective way of reducing water loss. Most drippers cannot be used as subirrigation devices because they clog up too readily when in contact with the soil. With a little ingenuity, however, soaker hoses, though designed for garden use, can be adapted to containers. For a large container, a length of soaker hose can be cut to encircle the inside of the pot, using an end closure so water seeps slowly through the hose. For small containers, use a large polyethylene-lined tray filled with sand in which the soaker hose can be buried. Then place individual pots on the sand, sinking their bases into it. The pots will absorb water from the wet sand by capillary action through the drainage holes.

The ultimate in water systems is automatic watering. You can set up your drip irrigation system, test it well, then leave on even a lengthy vacation, and still find your container garden in fine shape upon your return. Automatic watering devices are usually installed at

Top: Support clamps hold an irrigation line in place; clamps are closely spaced because the line runs in front of a door.
Bottom: A battery-operated timer automates watering of a container garden on a deck.

gation lines to lawn and in-ground gardens. Some systems include sensors that determine whether water is really needed before turning on the system.

Ideally, a drip irrigation system should be unobtrusive and efficient, and should keep plants healthy and growing to perfection. Some problems do come up, however, and it is best to know how to deal with them.

All drip irrigation systems require adjustment over time. As plants grow in size, for example, they require more water. One solution is to leave the system on for a longer period of time. If certain containers begin to require more water than others, replace the drippers with ones that provide a greater flow rate, or add extra emitters. As summer comes to an end, cooler temperatures and fewer hours of daylight reduce watering requirements. Turn the system on for shorter periods. If any containers still receive too much water, clamp off tubing or remove drippers, plugging any holes according to the manufacturer's instructions.

Although many modern drip irrigation systems include turbulence devices that help keep the system from clogging, periodic flushing, once or twice a year, may be required. Remove the end closure of both the main line and the branch lines and turn the water on full force. Flushing is especially important when the system has just been installed—dirt or debris may have entered the lines during installation. When individual drippers become blocked, try cleaning them thoroughly, or replace them with new ones. If this doesn't work, the blockage is in the tubing. Remove the blocked tubing, plug the hole, and install a new length of tubing. Check the filter periodically, and clean or replace it as needed.

Drippers clog rapidly if allowed to remain in contact with the soil mix. Use support stakes inserted into the pots to hold drippers one inch above the mix.

To prevent lines from being pulled out, use support clamps to attach them to the patio, structure, or ground. Clamps are available in various sizes to accommodate different diameters of lines. Any lines in direct contact with the soil can be buried to help hold them in place. Support stakes hold individual drippers firmly in place; stakes designed to be attached to surrounding structures hold misters and sprinklers solidly and at the proper levels.

the faucet end of the system. They range from a simple timer that turns the water on once a day or every few days for a predetermined period to a sophisticated computer system that not only can run drippers and misters separately, turning them on for various periods several times a day, but also can run other irri-

Finally, in areas where freezing temperatures can occur, it is best to drain the irrigation system in the fall and, if possible, disconnect it and bring it indoors for the winter.

Fertilizing

You need to pay closer attention to the fertilization needs of plants growing in containers than you would to those of the same plants growing in a flower border or in a vegetable patch. Because of the limited volume of a container, you must compensate for the small root area by feeding more frequently.

If the soil mix already contains fertilizer, more fertilizer doesn't need to be applied until three weeks after planting. If you need to water frequently after planting, start the feeding program earlier.

Because watering leaches fertilizers out of the mix, how often you water determines how often you should fertilize. A container garden requires more frequent watering and fertilizing than a garden in the ground. Moreover, since fertilizers leach from mixtures containing perlite faster than from those containing vermiculite, plants grown in a peat moss/perlite mix require even more frequent applications of fertilizer.

Fertilizers are made up of a mixture of minerals needed for plant growth, plus filler products that dilute the minerals so they won't burn plant roots. The exact concentration varies from product to product, and can be quickly determined by reading the label. The three main elements—nitrogen, phosphorous, and potassium—are indicated, in that order, through the three numbers on the label. A 10-15-10 fertilizer therefore contains 10 percent nitrogen, 15 percent phosphorous and 10 percent potassium. All three should be present in any fertilizer used for container growing, although a large proportion of nitrogen (30-15-15, for example) indicates a fertilizer best used for foliage plants, whereas one richer in phosphorous than in nitrogen (10-15-10 or 20-30-15, for example) is best for flowering and fruiting plants. For mixed plantings, you can't go wrong with a balanced fertilizer offering equal proportions of all elements.

Plants don't require a large amount of fertilizer at any one time, but they do need to be fed continually. Any fertilizing method used should take into account this need for regular feeding.

The most common fertilizers for potted plants are liquid or soluble ones, designed to be applied as you water. Although they are generally intended for a single monthly application, you'll get better results if you apply a weak nutrient solution each time you water. If you choose this method, use only one-eighth the amount of fertilizer called for by the manufacturer. That is, if the label calls for 1 teaspoon per gallon of water once a month, use $\frac{1}{8}$ teaspoon per gallon each time you water. Increase the proportion to one-fourth the recommended amount in a rainy climate where fertilizers are quickly leached out of the mix. In very dry climates, water abundantly with clear water once a month to leach out any excess fertilizer.

Time-release fertilizers are another popular method of meeting the nutrient needs of a plant. Most organic fertilizers also fall into this category. As the plant receives water, these fertilizers—available in three-month, six-month, and twelve-month forms—are released in small amounts. (Check the label for rate of application.) The easiest method is to use a time-release fertilizer mixed with the soil. Whatever fertilizer you use, be sure it is balanced and contains trace elements.

Fertilizing can easily be incorporated into a drip irrigation system. Simply attach a fertilizer applicator (be sure it's appropriate for your system) to the hose at the beginning of the system and add the recommended fertilizer. Applicators range from simple devices that draw the irrigation water over a special plant food tablet, which then dissolves very slowly and feeds the

Time-release fertilizers make the task of feeding containerized plants easier.

plants, to "injectors," tanks that mix and dilute fertilizers to exact proportions. Syphon-type fertilizer applicators can also be used. Be sure to add an appropriate filter to any system you choose, as undissolved fertilizer products can quickly plug up the drip tubes.

Vacation Care

Can your plants get along without you for a long weekend? For a week? Regardless of what watering system you use, a plant sitter, or a friendly neighbor who visits at least occasionally, is a good idea if you plan to be away for a week or more. Even the most sophisticated watering systems need attention. You can make the plant sitter's watering job less burdensome in several ways.

Move the containers into a single watering spot, where they will be protected from wind and direct sun. Sun-loving plants can take filtered shade for a week or two.

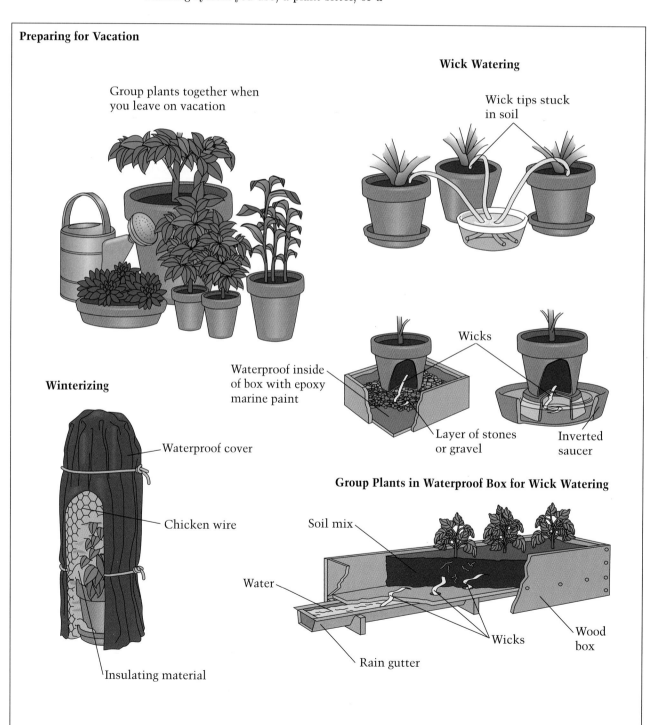

Preparing for Vacation

Group plants together when you leave on vacation

Wick Watering

Wick tips stuck in soil

Wicks

Waterproof inside of box with epoxy marine paint

Layer of stones or gravel

Inverted saucer

Winterizing

Waterproof cover

Chicken wire

Insulating material

Group Plants in Waterproof Box for Wick Watering

Soil mix

Water

Wicks

Rain gutter

Wood box

Wick watering can take care of containers for a week or more. Put one end of the wick in a pail of water and the other in the soil of the container. This gives the container a continuous supply of water. You can use a wick of glass wool, fraying the end that goes into the soil, or a nylon clothesline. Special plant wicks are also available.

You can build a two-compartment planter box for wick watering. The upper compartment holds the soil and plants; the lower compartment has a metal gutter that holds water with a nutrient solution for wick-watering and feeding the plants.

To create a water reservoir for a collection of wick-watered pots, you can use large custom-made pans of sheet metal, or homemade wooden boxes made watertight and filled with gravel.

Winter Protection

Protection is an important consideration if you live in a cold-winter climate. It can make the difference between survival and death for your container plants. You can protect vulnerable plants from the cold by enclosing both them and the container in a chicken-wire cylinder, filling the cylinder with insulating material such as hay, straw, or dried leaves, and keeping it dry with a waterproof cover. Make sure, though, that you keep the soil mix at least slightly moist: plants don't need much water during cold weather, but their roots must never dry out entirely.

Don't remove this covering too soon in the spring—frost damage can occur when balmy days are followed by cold windy nights. Just because a plant can survive the winter in the ground doesn't mean that it can manage cold weather in a container. If the garden soil in your area freezes, container soil will freeze even more solidly and the plants will probably die. This occurs because, unlike plants in the ground, plants in containers do not have the protective insulation of a large mass of soil surrounding their roots. If you live in the coldest northern zones, protect even hardy deciduous plants during the coldest months if they are left outdoors.

If your winters are not severe but still cold, make the most of the mobility of the containers and move them to protected areas during cold weather.

CHOOSING CONTAINERS

The sky is the limit when it comes to the containers you'll be able to use in your "movable garden." Everything that offers a planting space or pocket into which you can insert a few fistfuls of soil—pots, flower boxes, redwood planters, even old garden boots—will do. Your choice will depend on what is available

There are lots of pots to choose from, starting with clay containers of many sizes and shapes.

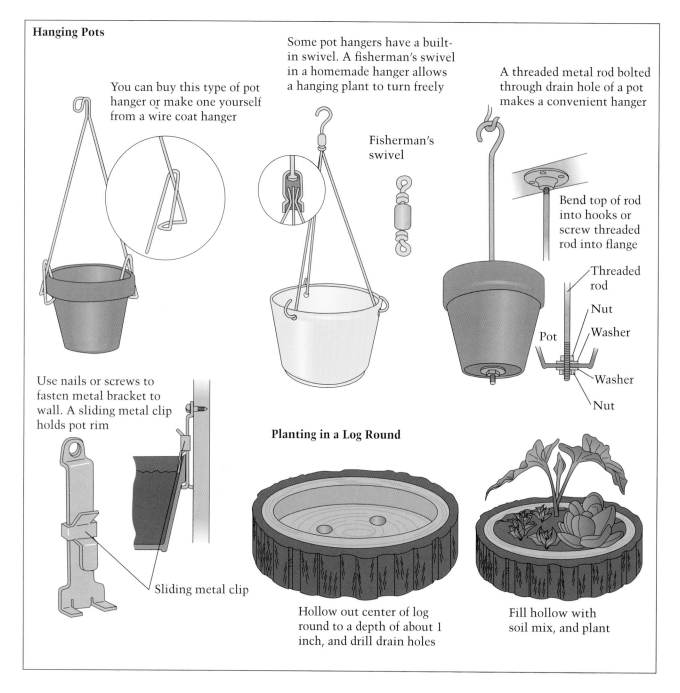

Hanging Pots

You can buy this type of pot hanger or make one yourself from a wire coat hanger

Some pot hangers have a built-in swivel. A fisherman's swivel in a homemade hanger allows a hanging plant to turn freely

Fisherman's swivel

A threaded metal rod bolted through drain hole of a pot makes a convenient hanger

Bend top of rod into hooks or screw threaded rod into flange

Threaded rod

Nut

Washer

Pot

Washer

Nut

Use nails or screws to fasten metal bracket to wall. A sliding metal clip holds pot rim

Sliding metal clip

Planting in a Log Round

Hollow out center of log round to a depth of about 1 inch, and drill drain holes

Fill hollow with soil mix, and plant

and the style you wish to incorporate into your container garden.

A visit to any garden center or lawn ornament specialist will reveal hundreds of possibilities: urns, strawberry jars, old stone feeding troughs, metal cauldrons, half barrels, watering cans, statuary with incorporated planting holes. You'll find other usual yet functional offerings in hardware stores, import stores, and kitchen specialty shops: buckets, kettles, wastepaper baskets. You will even find plenty of choices in and around your own home: old flowerpots, plastic-lined baskets, hollowed-out logs, tin cans, and many more.

Containers must offer enough root space for the plants they are to hold. Very small planting pockets can cause problems because they dry out so quickly that keeping up with the watering needs of the plants is almost impossible. The deeper and wider the container, the more soil it will hold and—since soil absorbs moisture—the less frequently you will have to water. The least expensive commercial flower boxes, for example, are often very shallow and narrow, and maintaining established plants in them is difficult without watering several times daily. Wider, deeper models are available and make much better choices.

An equally wide range of materials, all offering different advantages and disadvantages, is used for containers. The ideal container holds water well enough to prevent plants from drying out too readily, yet is permeable enough to allow good air circulation: roots, after all, need to breathe to do well. It is also insulated enough to protect plants from extreme temperature changes. In most cases, lightweight containers are best, as they can be moved more easily than heavy containers. In very exposed sites, though, heavy containers that won't topple over in heavy winds may be preferable.

Earthenware pots, either the ornate Italian ones made in a variety of forms or simple, straightforward flowerpots, are available in a wide choice of sizes. Their permeable sides offer good air exchange, but the trade-off is increased water loss, making them poor choices for dry climates or moisture-loving plants. Using a relatively heavy soil mix with a small proportion of vermiculite and perlite will help reduce water loss. Clay pots are also quite heavy, and poor-quality ones may crack in extremely cold weather. They do provide excellent insulation, however, keeping plant roots cool on searing days. Always soak new clay pots in water overnight before use; otherwise they'll absorb it from the roots of the plants you're trying to grow.

Ceramic pots made of glazed clay come in such a wide array of colors, forms, and sizes that there is almost no limit to the possibilities. Like clay pots, they are heavy; unlike clay pots, they are impermeable, thus requiring a lighter soil mix and less frequent watering.

They are also less subject to frost damage, but it would be wise to bring valuable ceramic containers into a frost-free room or cold frame for the winter.

Concrete and stone containers are perhaps the ultimate in outdoor gardening containers, at least as far as appearance is concerned; few other products quite match their elegance. They keep plants cool in the hottest weather and breathe well, yet are not so permeable as to lose much water to evaporation. Quality products are so crack-resistant that they may well outlive you! Their extreme weight makes them poor choices for balconies and rooftops, but they're naturals for ground-level gardens. Stone containers are nearly impossible to find other than in stores specializing in antique garden ornaments, and can be very expensive. Concrete containers, however, imitate them so well that it is hard to tell the difference. They are widely available and relatively inexpensive.

The variety of plastic pots is practically infinite. Far from the traditional green flowerpot, today's molded plastic can imitate anything from wood tubs to Grecian urns, all in the color of your choice. Plastic with a matte finish is used by some manufacturers to produce pots that imitate terra-cotta, without the stains. Plastic is lightweight, strong, and frost resistant, although inferior types may crack or discolor under prolonged exposure to sunlight. Probably its only flaw is that it is not porous and therefore limits air circulation. Make sure you use a light, airy soil mix with plenty of perlite and vermiculite to compensate. Because of their all-round usefulness, wide availability,

Left: Sturdy concrete containers are practical except where weight is a consideration. Right: Colorful glazed ceramic containers reduce the need for watering.

For variety of container appearance, wood can't be beat. It can be made into many shapes, including custom designs to fit a particular space. Redwood offers rustic, rugged good looks; less expensive wood can be painted or stained to match the house or to carry out a complementary color scheme.

and great variety, plastic planters are the first choice of most container gardeners.

Wood is second in popularity among the materials used for outdoor containers. It offers excellent insulation from hot temperatures, and good air circulation and water retention. Its natural appearance means that it goes with almost any decor. Unless carefully chosen, however, wood planters tend to rot quickly when filled with soil. Redwood and cedar are among the best kinds of wood for container use. They resist rot relatively well and weather attractively without paint or stain. They are, however, quite expensive. Inexpensive wood planters are widely available, but are rarely made of rot-resistant wood. They should be treated with a copper-based wood preservative. Do not use creosote or wood preservatives containing pentachlorophenol since they are toxic to plants. Painting, staining, shellacking and other treatments also help make wood planters impermeable and therefore extend their useful life.

Wood is ideal for making your own planters. For best results, used air- or kiln-dried redwood or cedar, or pressure-treated lumber. Less expensive wood, such as exterior-grade plywood, is also a good choice, especially if you treat it with a copper-based preservative. When applying the preservative, remember to seal the edges.

Elevating Containers

Containers should not be set directly on a flat surface because the constant contact between the bottoms of the containers and the surface can block the drainage holes, leading to poor

growth and root rot. Also, if the surface on which the containers are placed is made of wood, such as a deck or balcony, it will remain constantly moist and begin to rot. Likewise, wood containers in direct contact with a moist surface will rot eventually. All planters, tubs, and boxes should therefore have air space beneath them. If the container you buy or build doesn't have casters or feet, use small wood blocks to keep the container an inch or so above the ground.

THREE SPECIAL KINDS OF CONTAINERS

Here are ideas for three specialized types of containers that can be combined with more conventional pots and tubs of soil to extend the dimensions, variety, and beauty of your container garden. The first offers a simple means of accommodating plants in even the most difficult spots; the second allows you to create an outstanding garden feature with unusual plants; and the third helps you to get your container garden off the ground—literally.

Pillow Packs

A pillow pack is a seasonal container made by filling a "pillow" with synthetic soil mix and planting it so that flowers and foliage hide the pack itself. The result is a dense mass of vegetation, from a single plant or a whole bed, in a flexible container. The pillow pack can be molded like putty to fit an odd-shaped cranny or to nestle securely on a surface too sloping or uneven to support a conventional planter. It is clean, it provides maximum space for soil and roots in a confined spot, and its soil stays put, even in a heavy wind.

A large pack, or a group of packs, can be placed in the corner of a balcony or small patio to form a mound of blossoms and foliage, softening the harsh angles of the planting area and suggesting the contours of a natural landscape. Packs can be used alone or in combination with pots, tubs, and boxes. Packs of various sizes can be placed in decorative planters, and they can be transferred easily from one planter to another to create new displays.

Ordinary kitchen-type plastic bags—vegetable bags, refrigerator bags, bread bags, or trash bags—are potential pillow packs. Or you can buy plastic tubes at a plastic supply shop. One of the simplest pillow packs comes ready-made: an unopened bag of commercial planting mix.

To make the pillow pack, fill the bag or tube with lightweight synthetic soil mix to within 2 to 3 inches of the top. Fold the plastic at each end and sew or staple the ends closed. Slit the plastic where the seedlings are to be inserted. Water with drip emitters inserted through the plastic.

If you hand-water, insert small open-ended cans, such as frozen-juice cans with both ends cut out. Use one or two cans in a small pillow, or one can about every 18 inches in a long tube. Punch small holes in the bottom of the pillow pack for drainage.

Water Gardens

Gertrude Jekyll, the famous English garden designer, considered water the "soul of the garden." Although she was writing about in-ground gardens, there is no reason why you can't introduce the special beauty of water to your balcony, deck, or patio container garden. You can create a large water garden that delights the eye with its beauty and the ear with the sound of moving water, or you can work on a smaller scale with a portable plastic tub only 2 feet in diameter. Even the smallest pool creates a magical focal point. A small plastic pool can be placed inside a more decorative container, such as a wine-barrel half, equipped with heavy casters for greater mobility. Grow your water plants in gallon-size plastic or clay pots and arrange them in the tub at varying heights by setting them on rocks or inverted pots.

Hardy waterlilies   Hardy waterlilies are perennials, dying back to their rhizomes each autumn and growing anew every spring. For best results, give them full sun—the more sun you give them, the better they'll bloom—and feed them regularly by inserting special waterlily fertilizer into their potting mix. They dislike currents and splashing water, so keep them away from fountains and waterfalls.

There are numerous hardy waterlilies in a wide variety of shades, but many become too large for tub use. Check with a nursery to find one that will suit the space you have available. Make sure you set the plants at a comfortable water depth for the variety you grow: some cultivars need only a few inches of depth; others prefer a foot or more.

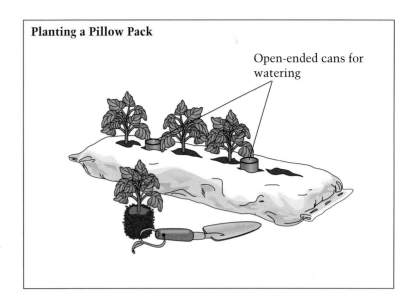

Planting a Pillow Pack

Open-ended cans for watering

In frost-free areas, plant hardy waterlilies at any time from February through October. Once the plants are established, they will winter over safely in the pool as long as the roots don't freeze.

In cold-winter areas, plant waterlilies at any time from April through August, when there is no danger of freezing. Except in the coldest climates, waterlilies will winter over if you cover the pool with boards and straw. If the winter climate is so cold that this method won't keep the pool from freezing solid, lift the pots after the first frost, when the foliage has

A water garden in a tub adds a delightful touch to a container garden.

begun to die back, and store them in a cool cellar. Keep the soil moist, or dry rot may attack the roots.

Tropical waterlilies   These tender waterlilies have so many blooms and are so beautiful that they are worth a little extra effort. Set them out only after the nights are warm—about May 15, depending on your location. Only in very mild climates can tropical waterlilies be left in the pool all winter. Elsewhere, take the bulbs out after the lilies have gone dormant and store them in a can of moist sand in a frost-free cellar or garage until May, then plant them.

Other water plants   A wide variety of other aquatic and semiaquatic plants can turn a simple tub or barrel into an enchanting garden pool. Upright-growing plants such as cattails (*Typha*) and bulrushes (*Scirpus*)—dwarf varieties of these are preferable in small containers—lend some height to the arrangement. Lower-growing plants such as parrot feather (*Myriophyllum aquaticum*) and water pennywort (*Hydrocotyle vulgaris*) dip over the edges of the tub, softening its lines. Floating plants, such as shell flower (*Pistia stratiotes*) and water hyacinth (*Eichhornia crassipes*), help shade the water, preventing algae growth while filtering out impurities and providing hiding places for fish. You can even grow lotus (*Nelumbo*), with their round, plate-shaped leaves and giant, colorful flowers, in containers as long as you choose small varieties.

Pool balance   For a successful container water garden with clean water free of insects, you'll have to create a mini-ecosystem all your own. The following four elements are needed.

1. Oxygenating plants, although submerged and therefore not very visible, are important for replenishing oxygen. Many varieties are widely available from water garden specialists.

Clean Water Formula

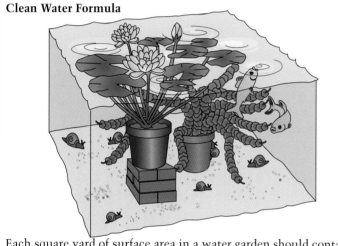

Each square yard of surface area in a water garden should contain the following: oxygenating plants: 2 bunches of 6 stems each; waterlily: 1 medium to large plant; snails: 12 ramshorn or trap-door water snails; fish: 2 fish, each 4 to 5 inches long

Hanging planters can provide a dramatic focal point and a splash of color in any garden.

Canadian pondweed (*Elodea canadensis*) is one of the best choices for containers.

2. Waterlilies are essential—their pads provide surface coverage, preventing loss of oxygen and keeping the water cool.

3. Snails contribute by eating algae, fish wastes, and decaying matter, which otherwise encourage algae growth.

4. Fish eat such pests as aphids, flies, mosquito larvae, and other insects. Keep in mind, however, that overfeeding fish with commercial fish food drastically changes the water balance.

Hanging Planters

Planters that hang add a dynamic dimension to many landscaping arrangements. On decks and patios or inside such garden structures as arbors, gazebos, and pergolas, hanging planters can highlight interesting details and disguise unattractive ones. They can also help define the space visually. If they are lightweight—and they should be—they can be moved from place to place indoors or outdoors for special occasions. Where space is limited, hanging planters may be a necessity. You can accommodate

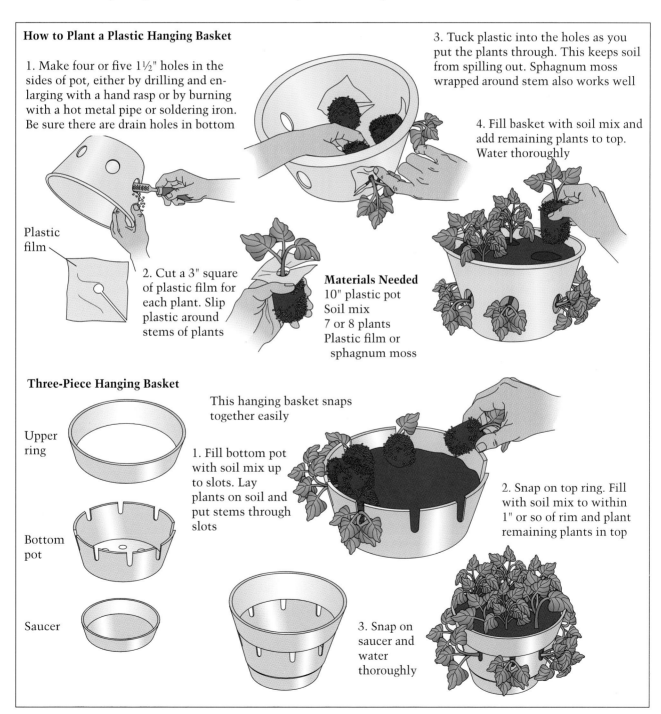

How to Plant a Plastic Hanging Basket

1. Make four or five 1½" holes in the sides of pot, either by drilling and enlarging with a hand rasp or by burning with a hot metal pipe or soldering iron. Be sure there are drain holes in bottom

Plastic film

2. Cut a 3" square of plastic film for each plant. Slip plastic around stems of plants

3. Tuck plastic into the holes as you put the plants through. This keeps soil from spilling out. Sphagnum moss wrapped around stem also works well

4. Fill basket with soil mix and add remaining plants to top. Water thoroughly

Materials Needed
10" plastic pot
Soil mix
7 or 8 plants
Plastic film or
    sphagnum moss

Three-Piece Hanging Basket

Upper ring

Bottom pot

Saucer

This hanging basket snaps together easily

1. Fill bottom pot with soil mix up to slots. Lay plants on soil and put stems through slots

2. Snap on top ring. Fill with soil mix to within 1" or so of rim and plant remaining plants in top

3. Snap on saucer and water thoroughly

To make sphagnum-moss basket, immerse the moss in a pail of water. Working with a handful at a time, squeeze out most of the water and press the moss around the top two wires (top left), pushing the first piece tightly against a vertical wire. Line the inside of the basket with overlapping pieces of moss (top right). Fill the bottom with 1½" of moist soil mix. From both sides, poke holes at soil level (center left). Insert plants through holes, with rootballs lying on soil surface (center right). Add another inch or two of soil and insert more plants until you reach the top. Stop about ½" below the rim, to leave space for watering.
Bottom: This hanging planter of blue and white Campanula isophylla *is turned weekly to keep it well rounded.*

many more plants by getting some of them off the floor, and also avoid the monotony of having everything on one level.

The simplest hanging planter is a clay or plastic pot suspended by a clamp-on hanger of wire or plastic or a hanger attached through holes in the pot. Some commercial handles have built-in swivels so that every side of the planter can receive sun.

A hanging container needs more protection from sun and wind than one that is on the ground. When the common clay pot is exposed on all sides to the movement of air, it becomes an efficient evaporative unit and requires a waterproof cover or much more frequent watering.

Many hanging planters are made of wood. The most durable are of redwood or other woods that are slow to decay. Wood is relatively lightweight, and many people find it very attractive. Plastic hanging baskets are also available in a wide range of sizes, forms, and colors.

Among the most useful and attractive hanging planters are moss baskets, heavy-gauge wire baskets usually lined with sphagnum moss. A well-planted moss basket is a showy living bouquet, a solid mass of foliage and flowers on the bottom, sides, and top. Some wire baskets are designed to be hung like pictures on wall brackets, rather than suspended. You can also hang a planter made from driftwood (see right). Another approach is the hanging cylinder or wall planter, made of heavy-gauge wire fencing and a perforated wood bottom, lined with plastic sheeting, and planted through slits cut in the sheeting. As the plants develop, the plastic disappears from view.

However you choose to put together your hanging planter, it's important to leave enough watering space at the top. Fill the planter with soil only up to ½ inch below the top, not up to the very top. Pack the sphagnum moss in thick and tight around the top inch of a moss basket. This creates a watering basin that allows the soil in the container to get thoroughly wet when you water, which in some cases should be daily or even twice a day. Use one heavy application of water to wet the soil, or you'll have to keep watering in small amounts three or four times a day in order to get a good soaking. You can also carry hanging baskets to a deep sink or a bucket and literally soak them in water for a few minutes to make sure they are thoroughly saturated. Obviously, moss baskets tend to drip for a while after watering, so hang them where this won't be an inconvenience.

Keeping the planter neat and in full color requires vigilant grooming. Remove all spent blooms. Prune off straying shoots. Pin shoots or vines to the moss with old-fashioned hairpins.

When frost or age has put an end to the good looks of a moss basket, take it to the compost pile or the work section of the garden and turn it upside down. Peel the layer of sphagnum moss off the root ball and save the moss and the wire for later use. Before building a new basket with fresh soil, clean the moss of any foreign material, soil, or plant roots.

Otherwise, care of a hanging planter is the same as for any other planter.

The following plants have drooping or trailing growth habits suitable for hanging planters. You can read about them in the upcoming chapters. This list doesn't exhaust all the possibilities, but it does suggest some of the most dependable and graceful plants for your hanging containers.

Planting in Driftwood

Handsomely twisted driftwood or tree branches make beautiful planters. Decide where you want the planting pocket. A concave area or the space between two or more branches is usually the easiest and most attractive place to plant.

Materials Needed
Driftwood
Chicken wire
Galvanized fence staples (staple-gun staples will rust)
Sphagnum moss
Soil mix

1. Cut and form wire to shape you want and staple it securely to wood. Leave opening at top for inserting moss and soil.
2. Line wire with sphagnum moss. Overlap pieces so soil can't leak out.
3. Fill pocket with soil mix and plant. Attach a heavy-duty screw eye so you can hang driftwood planter up.

Note: If driftwood comes from ocean, soak it in fresh water for several days to remove salt before planting.

Annuals and Perennials: asparagus fern (*Asparagus densiflorus*), basket-of-gold (*Aurinia saxatilis*), black-eyed-susan vine (*Thunbergia alata*), candytuft (*Iberis umbellata*), dwarf periwinkle (*Vinca minor*), Italian bellflower (*Campanula isophylla*), ivy geranium (*Pelargonium peltatum*), trailing lobelia (*Lobelia erinus*), verbena (*Verbena* hybrids).

Bulbs: orchid pansy (*Achimenes*), tuberous begonia (*Begonia tuberhybrida*, hybrids).

Cacti and Succulents (see page 56): burrotail (*Sedum morganianum*) ice plant (*Drosanthemum*), holiday cactus (*Schlumbergera*).

Herbs: mint, oregano, prostrate rosemary.

Shrubs: dwarf bougainvillea (*Bougainvillea* hybrids), camellias (*Camellia sasanqua* 'Showa-No-Sakae' and 'Shishi Gashira'), creeping cotoneaster (*Cotoneaster adpressus*), English ivy (*Hedera helix* varieties), hanging crape myrtle (*Lagerstroemia indica*), lantana (*Lantana* species), winter-creeper (*Euonymus fortunei*).

Designing With Containers

Like a poem, a container garden is a compressed form in which every element is important. To be pleasing, it can't be assembled haphazardly. Think about the effect you would like to have, and make a plan to achieve it.

A beautiful container garden isn't an accident. It is planned, perhaps not down to its tiniest details, but in concept, so a general intent guides its development. It has a coherence that says this garden has been thought out, no matter how diverse the elements that make it up.

Think about what you want your container garden to be. After all, there is no limit to the effects you can have. Would you like a quiet, cozy nook? Plentiful greenery—exuberant vines and hanging baskets of foliage dripping from every corner—and a modest quantity of flowers in carefully harmonized colors will produce a feeling of calm and tranquility. Do you want to create an impression of spaciousness on a postage stamp–sized balcony? Dwarf plants representing, in miniature, full-grown shrubs and trees, in an uncrowded arrangement, will impart an illusion of generous space in even the most restricted spot. Cool colors such as blue and green will seem to recede, so the remaining spaces look invitingly open. Would you like to warm a cool, shady courtyard? You may not be able to knock down the neighboring building that is blocking the light, but flowers and foliage rich in whites, grays, silvers, and pastel shades will pull sunlight, at least visually, into the darkest corner.

The design of a container garden is similar to the composition of a painting. Here, as in an old master's still life, a collection of succulents is framed by flowering plants.

A combination of geraniums and heliotrope illustrates basic principles of grouping plants in containers: a limited color scheme; frilly variegated leaves contrasted with smooth, solid-color foliage; the repetition of a matched set of pots on each side of a flight of stairs.

bloom, then the next week draw attention to some attractive foliage. The flexibility of the container garden is its main advantage. Don't miss out on this feature by assuming plants have to stay put.

The typical container garden, especially on a balcony or in a courtyard, has to be small. There isn't enough room to create a parklike look. But don't regard this as a limitation. Concentrate instead on suggesting a landscape through a condensed version of nature. For centuries Japanese gardeners have been masters of this art. In fact, capturing the spirit of nature—of the forest, the high country, or the seashore—is perhaps easier for the container gardener to accomplish in miniature than it is for the landscape gardener to achieve on a large scale. A well-placed small rock or two, some moss, and a small piece of driftwood can summon up the feeling of a natural landscape and set a mood for the rest of your container plants.

Whether or not you choose to plant in the style of the Japanese, it's worthwhile acknowledging and making use of their basic contribution—setting off plants, singly or in natural groupings. By arranging a stage for a few choice plants in the part of the garden you use most often, you get the greatest effect for the least amount of time, energy, and money.

GOOD PLANT COMBINATIONS

Not all plants belong together. A spiny candelabra cactus, with its stark, naked silhouette, will look out of place next to a luscious fern, and a tiny rock-garden iris will lose its charm when its nearest neighbor is a 4-foot shrub. For a harmonious arrangement, try to match a plant with a companion that is compatible in appearance.

For the strongest effect, select a narrow range of colors or just two colors. An all-white collection is a gardening classic. A blue-and-white combination is cool and refreshing.

Textures are just as important as colors. Include a bit of variety, such as fine-leaved, airy plants and large-leaved, coarser ones, to create interest.

A good idea is worth repeating—at least on a small scale. Recurring colors, forms, and textures in two or three containers will help to draw the garden together.

Remember that colors in a garden regularly change. The light, bright apple greens and pastel shades of spring give way to the more sober greens and strong yellows, pinks, and blues of summer. These cede their dominance to the golden hues, scarlet reds, and rich ochers of fall. Winter brings a blanket of white or a landscape of grays and brown, which may be enlivened by elements that create or suggest movement. Take advantage of these seasonal changes to make your container garden appealing throughout the year.

The beauty of traditional gardens, in which plants are rooted firmly in the ground, tends to wax and wane. This need not occur with container gardens. Because nothing is permanently fixed in place, you can mix, match, and move plants, constantly re-creating your mini-landscape. Cluster plants together, or move them apart; one week, focus on something that is in

Grouping Containers in an Arrangement

A very basic container garden might include just one tub or a single window box, but most tend to grow over the years as their owners gain horticultural skills and confidence in their designing ability and as they discover the pleasures of container gardening.

Although you can—and should—use your imagination in choosing containers for your expanding container garden, try to pick ones that will go well together by sharing a theme, texture, form, or palette. After all, the end result should be a stylish and innovative garden, not an eclectic collection of planters. Wood planters stained the same shade or various earthenware pots, though they are of different sizes and forms, will tend to unify the arrangement. Even a garden composed entirely of plants grown in a diverse collection of pots, kettles, and tin cans can have a pleasing homey effect, the common thread being that all are kitchen containers.

Some container gardens call for rigid placement and perfect symmetry that imitate a formal French or Italian garden but on a smaller scale. These gardens are, however, few and far between and furthermore are very hard to develop. Most successful container gardens are informal in style because of the variety in the containers used and the plants they contain. It would be a mistake to arrange such gardens

To be successful, a garden design must have variety—under control. The grouping above features different plants with varied shapes, colorations, and elevations; control results from similar scale and pot material. The design at left, with an assortment of plants at different heights, moves in a curve down the steps; control is exercised through the almost-monochromatic color scheme and, again, pot materials.

too severely. A better approach is to create a natural flow or rhythm.

To do this, group certain containers closely and space others farther apart. Use hanging plants that draw the eye downward to linger and admire the beauty of the understory plants; a climbing plant that stretches upward will bring the eye full circle. Follow your natural inclination to put tall plants in the back and sides of the arrangement, shorter ones in the front, and intermediate ones in between, but don't be too rigid in your composition. Why not insert an element of surprise by letting a tall plant rise out of a cluster of low-growing plants?

Just as the plants vary in height, so should the pots. Putting them all on the same surface of a deck or balcony will look all right, especial-ly if the pots are dissimilar. However, you can energize the arrangement by raising some of them on rocks or inverted boxes and placing one or two on pedestals. If you have available wall space, you can attach planters to it, adding vertical dimension to what is often a two-dimensional display.

To create further interest, consider adding a statue, an unusual rock, a shapely piece of driftwood, or another strictly ornamental element. Then give this element mystery by placing it partly out of sight.

Of course, thousands of possible combinations are appropriate for even the smallest garden, so don't hesitate to move containers and ornamental objects around whenever the inclination hits you.

Grouping Plants in a Single Container

In the same way that you strive to turn your limited growing space into a container garden, you can try to create a garden within a single container. There is no rule that says each container should hold only one plant or one type of plant. Large containers especially—tubs, planters, window boxes, broad trays—can easily become miniature landscapes of their own.

In creating a garden within a tub or tray, keep in mind the principles that guide preparation of a garden composed of many containers. The plants should be compatible in scale, offer a pleasing combination of forms, colors, and textures, suggest a certain amount of movement, and have a focal point that directs the eye. The design goal is to strive for harmony with just enough contrast to create interest.

A low tray is the ideal container for a miniature landscape: alpine plants seeming to grow out of rock face, or a spring garden of mosses and miniature bulbs re-creating a mountain meadow. Cactus and succulent gardens can likewise imitate the desert: tiny creeping succulents, a few spiny, upright cacti, some shrubby succulents of intermediate size, and a well-placed selection of rocks. You need little more than this to create the desired effect.

It is very important that all plants growing in the same container have similar needs. While it is easy to grow a tub of waterlilies next to a pot of cactus, it is nearly impossible to grow them in the same planter. Watering needs are the foremost consideration: group plants

Top: A white pine bonsai creates a mini-landscape in a tray. Bottom: A trough garden brings together cacti and succulents.

according to whether they prefer or can at least tolerate dry soils (most succulents) or they prefer soil mixes that never quite dry out (most other plants). Consider also any other special soil needs. It would be difficult to create a tub garden featuring acid-loving rhododendrons and plants preferring a regular pH, unless you use the pot-within-a-pot method described below. Light needs should also correspond, although it is still relatively easy to combine plants that need full sun with those that require shade, by placing the container so the former are on the sunny side and their counterparts are on the shady side.

Mixed tub plantings are usually permanent, at least for the season. In large containers, however, you can still include temporary plantings using the pot-within-a-pot method. Insert an empty pot of appropriate size (about 6 inches) as you plant the container in the spring. Then, throughout the season, you can easily insert 6-inch pots of colorful plants and remove the plants when they cease blooming.

Rotating to Take Advantage of Peak Beauty

The mobility of container plants lets you display new color almost instantly, the year around. A container garden need never have a dull season. For example, early bulbs, flowering quince, camellias, and primroses can be moved aside as petunias, sweet alyssum, dwarf marigolds, delphiniums, summer vegetables, and other late-spring and summer plants come

If a Planter Is Too Heavy to Lift

To move heavy planters and boxes, use a dolly, casters, or rollers of pipe or wood dowels 2 or 3 inches in diameter

Hand truck with trash bag for garden cleanup

Permanent or temporary feet keep container bottoms off ground

A table creates a small holding area for seedlings, cuttings, and out-of-bloom plants. In the frog-shaped vase are extra drip-irrigation parts.

into season. A few months later, these too can be moved into the background as dwarf crape myrtle and chrysanthemums begin to flower and the berries of pyracantha and Japanese barberry color brightly. The vibrant autumn foliage of dogwood, Japanese maple, and Washington thorn can transform the late-season garden. Plants bearing bright berries can dress up the garden well into winter, backed up by such dependable evergreens as Japanese black pine, holly, and dwarf Alberta spruce.

Maintaining a holding ground   Because every plant in a container is spotlighted, a planter of perennials out of bloom, a pot of bulbs whose flowering has ended and whose leaves are beginning to wither, or a boxed shrub just pruned radically can stand out glaringly in a container garden. So it's a good idea to establish a holding ground, even if it is just the least visible corner of a balcony, where plants can stay until they are ready to return to a focal spot. This ability to move plants into view when they look their best and to make them disappear when they are no longer attractive is one distinct advantage container gardeners enjoy over those whose plants are established in the ground.

The holding ground is the ideal spot for starting new cuttings or seedlings, for planting bulbs, and maintaining plants with strictly sea-

sonal periods of interest. Ideally, the holding ground should be in a sunny spot, as bright light helps plants recuperate fast. If your container garden is a shady one, the holding ground can become a flower nursery. Use it to give plants ideal conditions until they reach full bloom. They can then go into the shady but focal part of the garden and still maintain their brilliance for long periods. The same plant grown in constant shade might never have bloomed at all.

The holding ground can be especially useful for reviving tired annuals. Remember that the life objective of all plants is to produce seeds. Annuals must accomplish this in a single growing season. Fading flowers signal the beginning of seed production. At this time, much of the plant's energy is diverted from the production of new stems, leaves, and flowers and channeled into seed formation. To keep the plant flowering, remove the fading flowers by pinching or cutting them back ½ to 1 inch below the old flower head. If the plant has more seedpods than flowers, don't throw it away. Move it to the holding ground. Cut it back, fertilize and water it, and watch it start all over again. Petunias, snapdragons, and verbena, among others, respond well to this drastic treatment.

Bringing the beauty inside   While planning your container garden, consider adding extra pots for eventual use indoors. After all, why not take advantage of nature's bounty to create an interesting and colorful temporary display inside your home? The advantage to bringing living, potted plants indoors in their prime, rather than simply preparing a vase of cut flowers, is that the blooms are longer-lasting—up to a month in most cases. Even better, the plants are recyclable: they can be moved back outdoors to recuperate and will soon be in bloom again.

BALCONY AND ROOFTOP GARDENS

Perhaps the greatest challenge to the container gardener—and the greatest feeling of satisfaction as well—comes from designing a garden for a spot where a garden was never intended: a balcony or a rooftop.

These sites are often much hotter in summer than nearby courtyards because there are few, if any, nearby trees to provide protection from the sun, which brick, asphalt, or cement surfaces collect and reflect. These sites are also vastly colder in winter, because there is not a deep layer of soil to moderate temperature changes.

The solution to many of these problems comes from the very plants you grow and the containers in which you grow them. A deep planter or tub holds enough soil to moderate the worst temperature extremes and enough water to cool the air at least slightly on hot days. The plants grown in them also moderate temperature, via the water that they give off through evaporation, and buffer winds, which are softened as they pass through the foliage. Nevertheless, plants in containers on balconies and rooftops undergo more stress than the same plants rooted in the ground. It's up to the container gardener to make their life as easy as possible.

A Rooftop Garden Without Containers

Occasionally, one sees rooftop gardens without containers: soil mix simply has been spread over the surface of the roof. Since many roofs have ridges on the outside perimeter, this solution might seem logical. The problem is what to do when leaks occur, and leaks do indeed occur over the life of an average roof. Removing the soil, finding the leak, and drying out the surface so repairs can be made make rooftop gardening without containers somewhat hazardous. If you want to take the risk (and it has been done successfully) cover the surface with heavy, leakproof plastic and make sure that the drainage areas don't become clogged.

Very few roofs have been designed specifically with planting beds in mind. If you're lucky enough to have access to one, you can garden there to your heart's delight.

Choosing Plants

Plants in containers on rooftops and balconies suffer from more heat, greater cold, and stronger winds than their soil-grown counterparts. Therefore, it is wise to choose only the toughest ones, especially on the outside edge of the container garden, the part most exposed to the elements. Avoid plants with fragile branches that may break on windy days or be torn to shreds by brushing constantly against hard surfaces. In choosing hanging plants for a

Containerized plants make a balcony garden possible.

windswept window box, for example, select those that arch outward, away from nearby structures, rather than those that hang straight down and thus risk constant friction as winds push them against nearby walls. Any plants considered delicate—such as ferns, woodland plants, and weeping trees—should be either passed over or planted on the *inside* of the container garden, not at its edges.

Many balcony and rooftop gardeners have difficulty wintering plants over and therefore stick to annuals, houseplants, and temporary plants for their green spaces. This need not be the case. Obviously, container plants in such an exposed site cannot be adequately protected from cold winter temperatures. But by choosing plants capable of surviving temperatures at least 20° F lower than the lowest temperature expected in your area, you can have permanent plantings that will do wonderfully in even the worst cold. If, in your area, the average annual minimum temperature is 0° F (this corresponds to USDA Zone 6), you should select plants capable of surviving -20° F, or two USDA zones hardier (USDA Zone 4). You'll be able to find extrahardy trees, shrubs, vines, and perennials that can survive in Arctic conditions (see the individual plant descriptions in the fourth chapter for dozens of examples). They should do well in exposed containers in all urban areas in North America.

The disadvantage of using hardy plants in elevated gardens is that even the toughest ones will not survive in small containers. An 18-inch by 18-inch container is about as small as you can go and still offer enough soil to buffer temperature extremes. This means a trade-off between a container that is lightweight and one that ensures the hardiness of the plants. You really can't have both. Try a compromise: one or two large containers or tubs of shrubs or small trees used as permanent plantings, combined with smaller, lighter containers of annuals, vegetables, or other temporary plants for seasonal color.

Providing Shade

Sun-drenched asphalt roofing shingles become so hot you can practically cook an egg on them. This is *not* something your plants are going to appreciate. This is truly full sun—too much of it for even those plants that need full sun. After all, even sunny spots in a garden get a bit of shade from trees and shrubs during the day.

If possible, install a pergola or arbor partially covered with shade cloth (available from greenhouse suppliers), bamboo screening, or latticework on a rooftop garden to provide shade for at least part of the surface. Such a structure will be doubly efficient, acting as a windbreak at the same time. Not only will the plants directly under the structure get filtered light, but, as the sun crosses the sky, the shadows of the structure will offer some shade to parts of the roof garden to the east, north, and west.

Water Problems

The first difficulty with watering plants on a balcony or rooftop is getting water to the site. Several solutions are offered in Hand Watering on page 19 and in Drip Irrigation on page 20. Drip irrigation is especially recommended for rooftop gardens, where hot temperatures and lack of shade create a need for watering twice a day.

Another difficulty is constant dripping after a heavy rainfall. Balcony and rooftop surfaces normally drain rapidly, but excess water slowly draining from a large container can continue long after the rain has stopped, creating slippery conditions and annoying any neighbors below. Start by using an appropriate soil mix. Also, raising containers off the floor of the bal-

cony or the rooftop on wood blocks (see Elevating Containers, page 28) speeds up drainage considerably. If this isn't sufficient, slide waterproof trays under the containers to catch any runoff. This is easy to do if the containers are raised on blocks. The trays can be emptied into a sink or used to water the plants when they begin to dry out after the rain.

Weight Problems

When gardening on a balcony or roof, there is an important safety aspect to consider: can the structure support the weight of the container garden you hope to install there? Fortunately, balconies are designed to support a considerable amount of weight. Most have small surface areas and are amply supported, often at all four corners. Using lightweight soil mixes and avoiding containers made of very heavy materials such as stone or cement should provide the security you need.

Rooftop gardens are a different story. How much weight they were designed to support depends largely on local building codes for live loads, which in turn are based on expected charges, usually snow cover but rarely gardens. In some areas, 30 pounds per square foot is the norm. Yet live loads vary widely from municipality to municipality, and also depend on the building code in effect at the time a building was constructed. Check with the building department to find out the maximum charge and try to remain well under it. Although you may feel that your container garden will be well below the live load, don't forget to check, before starting your project, how much weight wet snow can add to already-soggy winter soil.

In rooftop gardening, use the lightest soil mixes possible. You can also reduce weight by using shallow containers wherever possible. To cover 50 square feet of planting space with 16-inch-deep containers, for example, you need 67 cubic feet of soil mix. If the containers or boxes are only 8 inches deep, you need only half that amount of soil. This means you'll have to water more often—all the more reason to consider installing a drip irrigation system. Remember, too, that shallow containers are unsuitable for permanent plants.

You can use heavy containers on a rooftop, however, if you place them carefully. Roofs have ample strength to support the heaviest containers directly over supporting walls and posts; the weak parts are between the beams. Study the roof carefully to discover where the main supports lie. Outer walls, which are simple enough to spot, can bear the weight of containers. Corners are the most solid places of all since they are formed of thick posts connected directly to the foundation however many floors below. Sometimes inner supporting walls are visible on rooftops as ridges, but more often they are hard to locate, as are the support beams that run across the roof. This is unfortunate, as beams too can support a great deal of weight. Locating them will help considerably in your planning since heavy pots can be placed so they rest on two beams, but not in between them.

If you're willing to foot the added expense, it is even better to design an open-slat wood deck over the existing roof. With the aid of an architect, who can properly plan the project, the supports for the deck can be firmly anchored to the strong points of the structure of the building. With a self-supporting deck, you can design the garden of your choice rather than limit the placement of plants to the strongest spots.

Coping With Wind

Any upper-story garden is subject to strong winds. The balcony or rooftop gardener faces a dilemma: how to reduce weight through light soils and featherweight containers, yet hold plants firmly in place? The solution is to anchor them solidly.

To prevent baskets suspended from an overhanging balcony from moving too violently, run a taut wire from the bottom of the pot to the railing below. Although thin wires are relatively unobtrusive as well as strong, you can always hide them partially by using them as supports for climbing plants.

To prevent tall containers from tipping over, screw the blocks that support them into the balcony floor and screw the bottoms of the containers into the blocks. You could also wire or screw the sides to a wall or to the railing. Do not, of course, in any way pierce a rooftop.

Window boxes—the long, narrow containers often used on window ledges and balcony railings—are of special concern. Although they seem heavy enough when filled with soil, it's amazing how much weight a strong wind can lift. For the greatest safety, place them on the floor of the balcony, inside the railing. Supports used to attach a box to a railing, wall, or window ledge (you'll find an assortment in garden centers and hardware stores) should be screwed into place. The container should then be screwed or wired to the support. To play it safe, in areas with heavy snow buildup, remove for the winter any window boxes attached outside a window or a balcony railing.

If possible, you should also incorporate a windbreak into your rooftop garden. A lattice-work wall or a row of containerized shrubs—choose only the hardiest—will go a long way in protecting main plantings from wind damage.

Lattice is an effective way to break the flow of air on a rooftop or balcony without creating destructive surges of deflected wind. The lattice can also mask a less-than-attractive view and provide some privacy.

Selecting and Caring for Plants

Choosing plants for a container garden is almost as easy as deciding what you like, and maintaining them is mostly a matter of following some simple guidelines.

Almost any type of plant can be grown in containers. Flowers—or what most people simply call "plants"—are beautiful in their own right. In containers, they can decorate the house or yard much as cut flowers do. Not only can they be arranged artistically within their containers, but individual containers can be moved around, or several containers can be combined in a display.

All foliage plants make good container plants, too. Hardy foliage plants can be left outdoors or in a protected place for the winter. Some of the tender houseplants—including most tropical houseplants—can decorate a patio or balcony during the warm months, and then be moved back indoors for the winter.

Vines make unusual container specimens. A pot of morning glories can be placed on a deck at the base of a string trellis. Perennial vines, such as clematis, can be grown in a container with a permanent trellis. They can spend the winter out of sight, then, when they come into bloom, be moved forward to provide shade or function as a screen for the summer.

Trees and shrubs, because of their size, make the most dramatic container plants. The natural dwarfing effect of growing in a container creates an appearance of great age in just a few years, much as it does with bonsai. A flowering cherry or star magnolia in a large container, stunning in bloom, can maintain its attractiveness when out of bloom because of this aged effect.

'Angelique' tulips and 'King Alfred' daffodils take well to container culture.

If you delight in fresh fruit right off the tree or tomatoes still warm from the sun, but live in an apartment with only a balcony as a growing area, you can still have a farm. With modern dwarf fruits and a wide range of vegetables bred especially for container culture, you can grow almost any of your favorite produce.

FLOWERS

Annuals, biennials, perennials, and bulbs are the principal, and sometimes the only, plants in a typical container garden. When confined to containers, they become movable flower arrangements. You can place the plants here and there, filling empty spaces as needed with the bright colors of pansies or petunias. You can also use them to highlight other plants or garden features or to call attention to a doorway. For instance, white impatiens can enliven a shady corner, and brightly colored geraniums or zinnias can make an entryway more inviting.

Other types of decorative plants are grown for their beauty, but are not usually thought of as "flowers." Although some cacti have beautiful flowers, most are grown for their structural beauty or novelty. Some flowering plants, such as morning glories, are vines and need special treatment and displays. Others, such as hostas or caladiums, have beautiful or colorful foliage and many of these make excellent and sometimes unusual container subjects.

Annuals

Annuals are plants that sprout, mature, bloom, and die within a single growing season. With so little time to grow, they waste no time, going from seed to flower in only a few months. They often bloom nonstop from late spring until fall, especially if you remove faded flower heads to prevent them from going to seed.

You can grow most annuals from seeds started directly in the outdoor containers in which you intend to grow them. In doing so, however, you miss several weeks of the blooming season: even the fastest-growing annuals take six weeks to come into bloom and therefore your containers will take awhile to reach perfection. It is much more practical to start annuals indoors in a bright window or under lights so that they are well established and possibly even blooming when the time comes to plant them outdoors (usually at or shortly after the last frost date in your area). An even easier solution is to buy pots or trays of annuals that are ready to be transplanted into your container garden. It is especially wise, unless you have a

Flowering annuals— 'Double Delight' and 'Fluffy Ruffles' petunias—combine with dusty-miller for a vibrant spot of color.

lot of experience with indoor gardening, to buy plants of those annuals that are slow to grow or are difficult to raise from seed.

Other than watering and fertilizing (see Watering, pages 16 to 23), annuals need little special attention once they have been planted. Any special requirements are indicated in the next chapter, where individual plants are discussed in detail.

Not all annuals are truly single-season plants. Some are tropical or subtropical plants that will live for several years in warm climates, but will survive only for one season in colder areas. In San Francisco, for example, zonal geraniums are perennials, but in Philadelphia, they are annuals. Plants treated as annuals in the fourth chapter are those usually grown as annuals in cold climates and considered as such by most gardeners.

Perennials and Biennials

If annuals are the stars of the container flower garden, designed for one brief summer of color, perennials make up the foundation of the garden through their durability and guaranteed performance. Whereas annuals die at the end of each season, perennials come back again and again, repeating their display every year.

Top: Perennials such as this chrysanthemum adapt well to containers. Bottom: This flowering container garden creates a riot of color and foliage on a deck.

They are generally defined as being nonwoody plants that endure season after season. Most die back to the ground in the winter, but a few remain green, offering a bit of winter color. Unlike annuals, perennials rarely bloom nonstop throughout the summer, and, instead, have specific periods of bloom. Therefore, a container garden using perennials changes constantly as one type of flower comes into full bloom, then relinquishes the spotlight to another.

The lifespan of a biennial falls between that of an annual and that of a perennial. Like annuals, they flower only once, dying after they have bloomed and produced seed. Unlike annuals, though, they don't bloom the first year from seed, but produce only foliage. In the second year, they burst into bloom, putting all their energy into a particularly spectacular flowering, as if they knew they had only one chance and this was it.

For best results with perennials and biennials in containers, purchase established plants or, for perennials, use divisions from an inground flower garden. Growing perennials and biennials from seed to bloom in containers, although possible, is a long process, as they don't begin to bloom until the second year, and most container gardeners want flowers the first season. Also, many perennials grown from seed do not produce blooms that are true to color. So the magnificent purple-flowered aster you try to reproduce from seeds may well give you everything from sickly white to pale lavender flowers. Only a few flowers will be close to those of the plant you wanted. Some perennials can be reproduced by cuttings.

Perennials and biennials can be planted together with other permanent plants, such as shrubs; you can put hardy bulbs in large containers to create a garden in a tub. All are also suitable for individual containers. Just move them to the forefront when they are in full bloom and put them in a less obtrusive corner when they have lost their charm.

The basic requirements of perennials are covered in the first chapter. They may need staking and regular cleaning to remove dead or dying foliage and flowers. Of course, after two or three years of container culture, most perennials become crowded and need division. If so, dig up the plants carefully and separate them into two or more sections before replanting. The extras can be used to start new containers.

The special needs of individual perennials are indicated in the following chapter.

Bulbs

No group of flowering plants offers brighter, more dazzling color than bulbs. Their flowers are the very essence of the late-winter and early-spring garden, but there are also bulbs that brighten the garden in late spring, summer, and fall. Massed in planters, bulbs make perhaps the most dramatic display of any group of plants.

Different bulbs require different treatments. Once you know their requirements, you can take full advantage of the opportunities that containers offer for growing and displaying bulbs.

Plan to use only a single variety, rather than mixed bulbs, in each container. Even within the same type of bulb, one color may bloom before another, and the resulting display, when in the spotlight of a single container, may be patchy and unattractive. Don't be stingy with bulbs—when planning a container arrangement, think in terms of masses of color, and plant the bulbs accordingly. If you want many colors, grow several containers, each with only one variety of bulb, for the most pleasing effect.

Your selection of containers is limited only by the number of bulbs you purchase, the depth of the pot (allow at least 2 inches of potting soil beneath the bulb for good root development), and the need for a drainage hole.

Containers can be as informal as a coconut shell or as classic as a clay pot. Bonsai containers lend themselves especially well to bulb display. Bulbs such as *Narcissus asturiensis*, the tiniest of the trumpet daffodils, are striking in a glazed bonsai container.

Once you've selected containers and bulbs, you're ready to plant.

Hardy Bulbs

Spring-blooming bulbs that are planted in the fall are known as *hardy* bulbs. Native to places that freeze in the winter, they begin to grow after the weather warms in spring. They are generally available in nurseries from late summer through winter.

Before you leave the nursery, make sure that each bulb variety is labeled properly. Buy a light commercial potting mix that will not become compacted, keeping permeability and

A collection of tender and hardy bulbs— joined by a primrose, in the foreground— produces flowers in profusion (top). The mass of blooms in each pot is achieved by planting bulbs shoulder to shoulder (bottom).

drainage in mind (see page 9). If you don't want to plant the bulbs right away, remove them from the bag they came in and store them in a cool, dry place. For outdoor container use, most spring bulbs can be planted in November or December.

When you're ready to plant the bulbs, take them out of their bags, one group at a time, and place them shoulder to shoulder in an empty pot, allowing a space of only ¼ to ½ inch around the outside of the group for soil. You may have to try several pots until you find one that fits, or may have to separate a large group of bulbs so they fit into smaller pots. For the best effect, at least three medium-sized bulbs or seven or more small ones, should go in each pot. Only the very largest bulbous plants are at their best when grown as individual specimens.

Using a waterproof pencil or pen on masking tape, label each container with the date planted. You can remove this tape at flowering time if it is too visible. Follow this procedure with each group of bulbs. To avoid mixing them up, concentrate on only one container at a time.

Keeping simple records is also practical. A small notebook will serve to record the necessary information for each container: name of bulb, date planted, date removed from cold storage, and date of flowering. Write down any additional details that might be helpful the following year. It's surprising how much you can forget from one planting season to the next. These records will help you establish a good blooming schedule in succeeding years and also will point up flaws in your original planning, so that you can repeat your successes and correct your mistakes.

Planting bulbs   Hardy bulbs need a period of chilling, followed by a period of root growth, before they are ready to bloom. Follow these steps to ensure the best blooms.

Step 1   Cover the drainage hole with window screen or curved pieces from a broken pot. This allows the water, but not the soil mix, to drain out of the container.

Step 2   Add a layer of soil mix deep enough that the tops of the planted bulbs will be 1 inch below the rim of the container. Placing the bulbs toward the top allows adequate room for root growth.

Step 3   Plant the flat end of each bulb—not the pointed end—facing down. If the bulb is planted upside down, it will right itself, but will take longer to grow, throwing off your gardening schedule and wasting the bulb's energy.

Step 4   Arrange the bulbs shoulder to shoulder in the pot, and gently firm the potting soil around them.

Step 5   Once the bulbs are in place, add enough soil mix to cover them.

Step 6   Water thoroughly by setting the container in a pail of water and letting it soak until the surface of the soil feels moist. Allow the excess to drain from the bottom of the container.

Step 7   Cover the pot with mulch. In very cold climates, this will keep it from freezing. In any climate, a mulch will slow evaporation and re-

duce the need for watering. Place the container where it is exposed to 12 to 14 weeks of temperatures between 35° and 50° F. This gives the bulbs the environment they need to develop a strong root system to support the production of shoots and flowers.

Step 8   Check the bulbs for moisture every few weeks, and water them as necessary to keep them slightly moist at all times. Hardy bulbs are not dormant when in cold storage, but are growing new roots and new shoots.

Step 9   At winter's end, or after 12 to 14 weeks of cold storage, the sprouts should be 2 to 5 inches high and the roots well visible through the drainage hole, indicating the bulbs are ready to bloom. When outdoor conditions permit, place the container in a holding area (if spring bulbs are coming up in nearby gardens, there should be no danger of severe freezing). When the flowers start to open, move the container to center stage so the blooms can play a starring role in your container garden.

Keeping bulbs cool   During the winter months, hardy bulbs need to be kept very cool, yet shouldn't be allowed to freeze deeply. In moderately cold climates, just leave the pots outside. To prevent freezing, put them in a box or trench and cover it with peat moss or a similar material. Shredded polystyrene makes an excellent mulch. It is lightweight, never freezes, and allows water to pass through readily. In severe winter climates, though, mulching may not be sufficient to prevent pots from freezing. Try putting them against a south-facing wall under a deep pile of leaves held in place with mesh, or in a cold frame warmed by a heating cable.

If all else fails, bring them indoors. An unheated cellar, cool attic, or cold room is ideal. An unheated garage attached to the house is also worth considering.

If you chill bulbs indoors, you may find they are ready before nature is. In this case, you have two choices: Move them to a location with warmer conditions and bright light and let them bloom indoors, which is called "forcing" the bulbs. Or, if you want to enjoy the showy blooms outdoors, keep the bulbs in cold storage, watering them as needed, until they can safely be put outside. The bulbs will remain in a sort of suspended animation until they are exposed to light and heat.

In climates where winters are warm, such as in the Deep South, "spring bulbs" are only something you read about in books or see on television. With container gardening, though, you can perform miracles. Just plant the bulbs in pots and refrigerate them for the required 12 to 14 weeks, and then place the containers outdoors when they are ready to bloom. Tulips in Florida? Why not!

After the flowers fade Even after the last petal has fallen from potted bulbs, you can keep the foliage in good health by providing moisture, sunlight, and fertilizer. Move the bulbs to a sunny, out-of-the-way place where the foliage can continue to mature, storing up strength for another year's blooms. When the

Staggered Blooms

Hardy bulbs grown in containers normally bloom at the same time as their garden counterparts or only slightly earlier. You can, however, considerably extend the bulb season by staggering their flowering times. To do so, when the pots are full of roots, simply store them in the refrigerator at 35° to 40° F until the flowering of the displayed pots begins to wane. Then move the refrigerated bulbs outdoors, pot by pot, over a three-week period. Using this method you can have narcissus, tulips, and crocuses in bloom well into June or even July, depending on the climate in your area. Most bulbs can be held in this way for as long as two months with no danger of deterioration.

How to Plant Bulbs in Containers

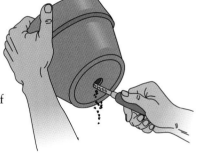

Check drainage hole and enlarge if necessary

Cover drainage hole with piece of window screen or broken pottery

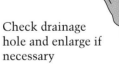

Partially fill container with planting mix

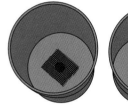

Plant bulbs, with flat end pointing down

Set container in a pail of water and let it soak

Cover container with loose mulch. If you have several pots, you can put them all together in a box

When bulb blooms have died, move the pots to the holding area, but continue to water and fertilize.

tion of a cold room, until the following year. You can also remove the bulbs from their pots and store them in dry sand, vermiculite, or peat moss. Start them again during the same period the following year. The bulbs often tell you they are ready to start a new cycle when, following an internal time clock, they begin to sprout on their own. Tender bulbs are very durable, and will bloom year after year in containers.

TREES AND SHRUBS

Growing trees and shrubs in containers is an ancient practice. Commercial nursery traders brought frankincense trees in containers from the Somali coast to Egypt about 3,500 years ago. Even before then—about 4,000 years ago—Egyptians grew trees in large "boxes" or "pots" cut into rock and filled with planting soil.

Today you can walk through nurseries and find countless plants that thrive in containers. In fact, all plants can be grown in containers, at least in the early stages of development. When you select trees and shrubs for container culture, it makes sense to choose dwarf or slow-growing types, which accept container conditions for years. The limited root space of containers, along with occasional pruning, keeps even the most vigorous shrubs and trees within bounds for a long time.

The list of plants in the next chapter includes trees and shrubs that are particularly effective in containers, but it is by no means exhaustive. The restricted root space in a container dwarfs any large plant. The dwarfing effect does not stem from the lack of space itself, but from the frequent stress of running out of water and, to some extent, food. As a tree grows larger, it quickly uses up the available water, then stops growing until it is watered again. This is the principle behind dwarfing trees such as bonsai; growth is slowed by frequent water stress.

Trees and shrubs that are adapted to dry soil, such as pines and junipers, are ideal subjects for container culture. But any tree or shrub can be grown in a container—as long as it is watered regularly.

Large plants call for some special considerations when grown in containers. One is the size and weight of the container. Large containers with large plants can weigh several hundred pounds, making them too heavy to move easily. If you can plan to locate a heavy

last leaf fades, move the container into a shed or other enclosed area so it can dry out thoroughly. (A very few hardy bulbs prefer *not* to dry out in the summer; these are noted in the individual descriptions starting on page 74.) Come fall, put the container outside again and water it well. Unlike bulbs forced indoors, which are so weakened by the heat and dry air of indoor conditions that they won't bloom the following year, bulbs grown in outdoor containers flower year after year. If the planting becomes too dense—and bulbs do multiply over time—divide the bulbs in the fall and replant them immediately.

Tender Bulbs

There is no special secret to planting tender bulbs in containers. They can be treated exactly as if they were in the ground, by planting them at the same depth and with the same spacing. Tender bulbs do not need a special chilling period, but begin growing as soon as they are planted. When they die back several months later, they should not be watered until the foliage dries up entirely. Then the foliage should be removed. During their winter dormancy, tender bulbs can be left in their pots in a moderately cool—50° to 60° F—dry spot, such as a cool basement or the warmest sec-

Bonsai

Bonsai, an ancient horticultural art form, represents an appreciation of nature in its many moods and settings—towering crags, luscious meadows, peaceful lagoons, rushing streams. The Chinese, then the Japanese, developed bonsai over many centuries; it is now an art commonly practiced in the West as well. Bonsai can be considered a special type of container gardening with trees and shrubs dwarfed by pruning and training to create living sculptures that reflect, in miniature, a segment of nature.

Bonsai are container plantings par excellence; their very name translates as "plant in a pot." In fact, a single bonsai can often set the tone for an entire container garden, the other plants and objects—decorative rocks, driftwood, bamboo screens, pedestals—being chosen to highlight the effect of the bonsai.

Bonsai have the same basic needs as other plants: water, air, fertilizer, and so forth. Because they live in an extremely restricted space, though, they require more constant maintenance and should be checked at least once a day. They must never dry out, for example, even if this means watering twice a day during hot weather. They also need protection from both overheating and freezing.

Contrary to popular belief, most bonsai are outdoor plants, although some may be brought indoors temporarily for display purposes or, in cold climates, for the winter. Even so-called indoor bonsai prefer to spend the summer outdoors where they can benefit from fresh air, good light, and temperature variations between day and night.

Bonsai are container plants by definition.

container in a semipermanent site, where the plant can reside for years at a time, the weight of the container is not a problem. If you wish to move the plant on a regular basis, keep it on a platform with casters.

Repotting is another concern. Plants that multiply their size many times during their life span need to be moved into a larger container several times, or at least until the plant is the size you would like it to remain. A plant's roots continue to grow for its entire lifetime. Once the root space is packed full of roots, there is little room for air or water. If the roots remain crowded, the plant will diminish in vigor and eventually decline. Periodic repotting is vital to the health of the plant. The best rule of thumb for repotting a large plant is to move it to a larger container when it needs watering almost every day. The next pot should be about 4 inches larger in diameter. Continue repotting until the plant is as large as you would like it to be. When it needs repotting, follow the procedure described on pages 12 to 16.

FRUITS AND VEGETABLES

When you start growing fruits, vegetables, and other edible plants in containers, you are joining a vast and expanding group of enthusiasts. Economy, recreation, ornamental value, and increased variety are a few of the many advantages of container gardening. Whether you already have an outdoor garden and want to take advantage of the convenience of growing a few edible plants in pots near the kitchen door, or you live in a house or apartment with only a balcony, patio, or roof area for gardening, you can develop your horticultural skills and please your palate with an edible garden in containers. Whatever your motives, if you've ever tried growing fruits or vegetables, you have discovered the superior flavor of a vine-ripened tomato or the tender sweetness of a freshly picked strawberry. Storebought produce can't come close to matching the quality of homegrown fruits and vegetables.

Grow zucchini one plant to a 5-gallon container.

Fruit Trees

Although many compact varieties of fruit have been developed recently for container culture, growing fruit in containers is nothing new. One of the most famous container-fruit gardens belonged to Louis XIV, who in the 1600s constructed an orangery at Versailles. The orangery, the predecessor of the modern greenhouse, allowed tender trees to produce fruit out of season. Some of the fruit trees at Versailles are said to have lasted 75 years. Of course, you don't need to aspire to such a grand scale as Versailles. Wherever you live, you can grow dwarf fruit trees that don't require a greenhouse.

The development of modern dwarfing techniques has reduced considerably the work required to grow trees in containers—dwarf trees are far less likely to become root-bound or to have problems with watering and feeding. Dwarf trees, both grafted and genetic, are discussed in detail below. First, here are some step-by-step planting and maintenance techniques that will keep your portable orchard healthy and productive for years.

As the Versailles garden shows, planting in containers allows tender plants to grow well far from their natural climate zone. You can move them to shelter when cold weather comes and wheel them to a shady spot when hot weather hits. Deciduous fruit trees do not need light when dormant and can withstand considerably lower temperatures than citrus trees can. Be careful not to overwater the plants while they are inactive.

Citrus trees are decorative enough to be brought into the house and placed in front of a south-facing window. You can put deciduous trees such as cherries and apples in a garage or in a basement cold enough to satisfy their chilling requirements. They will probably survive the winter there very nicely—but should be moved into the sun on fine spring days.

Any fruit tree theoretically could be maintained at a small enough size for container growing through harsh pruning of branches and roots, but it wouldn't be very productive. Genetic or grafted dwarfs naturally produce smaller, more numerous branches in a limited space, leading to a much improved harvest—and all with very little shearing.

What is your favorite apple? McIntosh? Golden Delicious? Cox's Orange Pippin?

Thanks to dwarfing rootstocks, you can have the apple of your choice in a container on your balcony. Standard apples are simply grafted onto dwarfing rootstocks that restrict the growth of the stem and branches without affecting the size or taste of the fruit. Malling 7, 9, and 26, for example—rootstocks developed at the Malling Research Station in England—all give varying degrees of miniaturization. For truly small apple trees, ones that can be maintained at only 4 to 6 feet in height, look for Malling 27 dwarfing rootstock. The size of pear trees can likewise be restricted by grafting onto quince roots. There are also many dwarfing rootstocks for citrus.

Genetic dwarfs—including apples, citrus, peaches, nectarines, apricots, and cherries—are plants that, by their very nature, are of small size. They make even better choices for container growing than grafted varieties, as they are more resistant to varying temperatures, are less likely to suffer breakage in bad weather, and often are more productive.

You can even obtain three or more fruit varieties grafted onto the same dwarf tree—for example, several apple or cherry varieties, or peach-nectarine-apricot or other combinations, all in one tree.

Begin your orchard with containers that are just 2 or 3 inches wider than the roots of the plants. If you start with a bare-root apple or pear or a genetic dwarf fruit, the first container should be about the size of a 5-gallon can. Since it will be in use for only one growing season, you might use a large tin can (the type cooking lard comes in) or a simple nursery pot, disguising it with a basket or box. Let the young tree grow for a season and fill the container with roots, then repot it into a more permanent home the following spring.

Evergreen fruit plants such as citrus should start out in containers that aren't too much

Dwarf citrus such as Nagami kumquat (left) and other fruit trees such as nectarines (right) make colorful and productive additions to the container garden.

Cacti and Succulents

Succulents are the camels of the plant kingdom; they have devised clever water-conservation techniques to carry them through periods of drought. As such, they are ideal plants for the container garden, very forgiving of the busiest schedule, repeated absences, or neglected watering. If you find handling other container plants a chore, or if you lose more plants than you save, succulents are the choice for you.

A few of the most popular are described here. Hundreds more, in a bewildering array, are available, and all grow well in containers.

Aloe vera (medicine plant): Very well known for the healing properties of its sap, this makes a striking addition to a container garden. It has dagger-shaped leaves in gray-green, lightly spined leaf edges, and irregular white markings. Young plants produce numerous offsets; mature ones tend to be solitary. Tall flower stalks of coral pink blooms are occasionally produced. There are many other aloes, ranging from low-growing dwarfs to tall, treelike types.

Crassula ovata (jade plant): A very popular treelike shrub with succulent, spoon-shaped leaves and a thick, multibranched trunk (previously known as *C. argentea*). The leaves take on a delightful reddish tinge in bright light. It grows to 4 feet with a massive, bonsai appearance in only a few years. Mature specimens produce clusters of white to pink flowers in winter. Widely available.

Drosanthemum (ice plant): There are several related ice plants, including plants from the genera *Lampranthus* and *Delosperma*. Commonly grown as ground covers in dry climates, these plants are often called "highway daisies" in California: their large, brightly colored daisylike flowers cover vast stretches along many roads. Their trailing stems and thick leaves look good in containers of all sorts, especially when covered in bloom. Multiply by cuttings.

Echeveria (echeveria): This varied genus of succulent rosettes is mostly ground hugging or on short stems, and is often cabbagelike in appearance. Some are grayish or bluish with a pink highlight, others have hairy leaves, and still others have deep green foliage with purple highlights. The leaves are usually smooth edged, but may be frilly or curiously warty. Bell-shaped yellow to red flowers may form on curled flower stems in spring. A good tabletop specimen.

Rhipsalidopsis (Easter cactus): Small, flattened, spineless segments arching down around a hanging pot and tipped with symmetric pink to red flowers characterize this popular cactus. Unlike most cacti, it does not come from an arid region, but rather dense, shaded rain forests. It needs protection from strong sun. Dry, cool conditions, as well as short days, are needed in fall to bring on spring flowering.

Rhipsalis (rhipsalis): Also a rain forest cactus, rhipsalis needs the same conditions as *Rhipsalidopsis*. There are many kinds, mostly with thin, stringlike segments or broad, flattened ones. Flowers are tiny and usually white. They are often followed by decorative, long-lasting berries, often translucent.

Schlumbergera (holiday cactus): This looks like *Rhipsalidopsis*, but is larger, has asymmetrical flowers, and blooms in fall and winter rather than in spring. For care, see *Rhipsalidopsis*.

Sedum morganianum (burro-tail): This very popular trailer has pale green spindle-shaped leaves densely covering stems that cascade to 3 feet in length. The rose-pink flowers appear in clusters at the tips of the stems, but are not often seen. Take care in moving this plant, for the leaves drop off at the slightest touch. Each fallen leaf, however, readily sprouts to form a new plant. There are literally dozens of other sedums, most of them tiny trailers forming small hanging baskets or ground covers for larger plants.

Sempervivum (hen-and-chickens): These ground-hugging rosettes of thick leaves form numerous offsets, creating veritable colonies in only a few years. Most have leaves with pointed tips. Most are smooth, but a few have a spiderweb appearance due to long, intercrossed hairs. They range in coloration from green to reddish to deep purple. Many are hardy plants and can be left outdoors in a sheltered location for the winter.

Cacti are a particularly good choice for the container gardener who has trouble keeping up with watering.

bigger than their rootballs. If the soil mix is well drained, use containers 3 or 4 inches wider than the roots. Large nursery plants can go straight into their final containers, the ones they'll grow in for the rest of their lives.

Permanent containers should be no larger than necessary so they won't be unwieldy, although you might consider a platform on wheels for any large container. A half barrel is about the right maximum size, as is any box or pot that holds about that volume of soil. Permanent containers should be no smaller than about 18 inches tall and 18 inches wide. The smaller the container, the more work will be involved in feeding, watering, and root pruning.

Since container trees must be removed from their pots every two or three years for root pruning, a homemade wood box that can be taken apart is perhaps the most practical container for fruit trees. Use screws to attach one side or, better yet, all four sides.

Move plants from the first (5-gallon size) container to a bushel-size container over two or three seasons. When a plant has an appropriately sized container, it can find water and nutrients easily. The right size also keeps soil from going sour around and beneath the roots, which slows top growth.

Feed fruit trees in proportion to how fast they are growing. They need lots of fertilizer in midspring, when they are growing rapidly. Feed less in summer, and stop about mid-July to give the new growth a chance to harden off. Plants that are moved indoors for the winter can be fertilized lightly the entire time they are in leaf.

Fruit trees should be repotted every few years, when they begin to need watering more than once a day or when growth slows, a sign that the roots have run out of space. Repot in the fall or early spring, when they are dormant. What is called repotting doesn't necessarily mean moving the plant to a larger container. Once a fruit tree has reached the maximum-sized pot that you can easily move on your own—say 15 gallons—it can stay in the same-sized pot indefinitely, but it will need to have its roots pruned—otherwise the feeder roots will bunch at the walls of the container and the plant will languish. Prune the roots by shaving off an inch of soil and roots around and underneath the rootball. Then place the plant back in its pot, filling in the empty space with fresh soil to allow the plant to grow healthy young

roots. When you prune the roots, always clip the top back a little to balance the plant. New top growth will follow as roots develop. After repotting, soak the soil thoroughly. Keep the plant out of full sun for a few days: this gives it time to produce a few new feeder roots.

Most fruit trees (figs are one exception) need to be pollinated by insects in order to produce fruit. If plants are outdoors in a place where they can be visited by bees, let nature take its course. Elsewhere, however, you may need to emulate the bee and do some pollinating. With a small artist's brush, transfer pollen from the stamen of one flower to the stigma (the end of the pistil, which protrudes beyond the petals) of another.

Many deciduous fruit trees are at least partially pollen sterile: they won't produce fruit unless fertilized by pollen from a different cultivar. For example, a 'Redfree' apple would need pollen from a 'Liberty', a 'Spartan', or even a crab apple if it is to produce fruit. If you don't have room for more than one variety of the same tree in your container garden, try buying a dwarf tree with more than one variety grafted onto it. You can also bring in a flowering branch of another fruit tree of the same

Many deciduous fruit trees need to be fertilized by pollen from a different cultivar. One way to get fruit from trees such as these dwarf apples is to be sure your collection includes more than one variety.

type and either leave it in a pail of water for the bees to discover or hand-pollinate using its flowers. Remember that fruit trees can only fertilize other trees of their category: apricots, for example, only pollinate other apricots, not pears. Most fruit trees are self-sterile. Ask a nursery or garden center to suggest those exceptions that are self-fertile varieties.

Citrus Fruits

Growing citrus fruit will certainly seem worthwhile when you breakfast on homegrown oranges, but the dwarf trees described here do have conditions that need to be met. They need direct sun at least half of every bright winter day; comfortable room temperatures; and moist, humus soil (equal parts of garden loam, peat moss, and sand). Give the plants a shower with tepid water once a month while they are indoors. Keep them outdoors during frost-free weather.

Citrus have special feeding needs. Special citrus fertilizers containing iron, zinc, and other minerals are available at nurseries selling citrus plants. Use these fertilizers regularly, or switch to them if you see signs of mineral deficiency, especially leaves with yellowed portions between bright green veins, when using your normal fertilizer.

Invest only in dwarf varieties developed specifically for containers. These will produce fragrant flowers the year around, as well as edible fruit. Some are genetic dwarfs, naturally small enough to remain in pots for their entire lifetime. Most, though, are standard-sized citrus grafted onto dwarfing rootstock (*Poncirus trifoliata* 'Flying Dragon' is a popular one). This means that any citrus can be dwarfed and grown in a container. When ordering container plants from specialized nurseries, be sure to insist they send you dwarf varieties.

Citrus are among the fruits that will need to be hand-pollinated if bees are lacking.

Small Fruits

A wide number of small fruits do wonderfully in containers. They are even easier to grow than fruit trees, as they naturally grow small. They thrive in small containers, making them easy to transport. Growing them in containers also allows you to elevate these ground-hugging plants so you can better appreciate their beauty—and you won't have to bend so low to harvest their delicious produce.

There are no special methods for growing small fruits in containers. Provide support for those, such as grapes, that need it. See the next chapter for information on specific fruits.

Vegetables

What could be more practical than being able to step out of your kitchen door and harvest your own fresh, ready-to-eat vegetables and herbs? It's not at all complicated, as most vegetables grow beautifully in containers.

When you grow vegetables in containers, you can take advantage of the various microclimates around the house and garden. For example, you might place heat-loving eggplant where it gets not only full sunlight but also heat reflected off a south-facing wall. Since vegetables are grown for their productivity, you can place them in spots where appearance doesn't matter, such as on a rooftop or fire escape.

Varieties in almost every category thrive and produce superior-quality vegetables in containers. As a rule, nearly all leafy vegetables take well to containers. Specially bred varieties of tomatoes, radishes, corn, and melons—virtually the whole spectrum of vegetables—yield first-rate crops in container gardens.

The standard growing techniques mentioned in the first chapter apply well to vegetables. Vegetables are particularly fast and easy to grow, most going from seed package to

This orange tree is a standard-sized plant grafted onto dwarfing rootstock.

kitchen table in only a few months. Most are started from seed sown outdoors, directly in their containers, once all danger of frost is past, although some frost-tolerant vegetables, such as peas and spinach, can be sown much earlier. Some vegetables, such as tomatoes, brussels sprouts, and eggplant, should be started indoors, about six to eight weeks before the planting-out date, to give them a head start on the season. In the spring you can also purchase transplants in pots or trays, all ready to go: just dig a hole, drop them in, and begin watering.

Herbs

A window box at least 8 inches deep makes an excellent patio herb garden. Individual plants can also be grown in pots. Chives, garden thyme, basil, marjoram, and summer savory do well in the confines of a planter box. The sprawling growth habit of the various mints, oregano, and prostrate rosemary make them attractive in hanging baskets. If you have room for 12-inch pots or tubs, you can add these to the list: tarragon, winter savory, upright rosemary, and a young bay tree.

For best results, grow marjoram, oregano, rosemary, sage, tarragon, and thyme in full sun, letting them dry out slightly between waterings. The following herbs should be watered more frequently: basil, burnet, borage, catnip, chives, comfrey, coriander, dill, parsley, and the various mints.

Minimum Container Depth for Some Vegetables and Herbs

Plant	Depth
Bush beans	10"
Pole beans	12"
Small beets*	8"
Round carrots	6"
Carrots to 8" *	12"
Chard	10"–12"
Cucumbers	12"
Eggplant	10"–12"
Lettuce	8"
Miniature leaf lettuce	6"
Scallions	8"
Parsley	10"
Bush and pole peas	12"
Standard peppers	12"
Compact peppers	8"
Radishes	6"
Summer squash	24"
Strawberries	8"
Tomatoes (tall)	15"–24"
Tomatoes (short)	12"–18"

*Don't attempt to grow large beets, or carrots longer than 8" in containers.

Potted herbs and edible flowers form a portable kitchen garden.

Plants for Containers

From the flower bed to the shrub border to the vegetable garden, from the longest-lived tree to the lettuce destined for this evening's salad bowl, there's a plant appropriate to container gardening. The instructions in this chapter will help you successfully grow more than one hundred of the most popular.

This chapter tells you how to raise some of the best plants of all categories for containers. The plants are in groups, with individual plants arranged alphabetically within each group. Once you've made your choices, purchase from a local source if possible. You can see exactly what you are getting, ask for advice when you buy, and return for help if problems develop.

You should find a good selection in a well-stocked garden center—in many categories. In some categories, however, the possibilities are so wide that a single outlet can carry only a sampling. If you can't find what you want locally, turn to the catalogs. Hundreds of nurseries sell plants and seeds by mail. They advertise in garden magazines, especially in the December and January issues. Call or write for catalogs to expand your choices.

The leafy grace of a Japanese maple highlights this container garden on a deck.

Ageratum houstonianum with *Lobularia maritima* and *Begonia semperflorens-cultorum*

Asparagus densiflorus 'Meyersii'

ANNUAL FLOWERS

Annuals are the easiest plants to grow from seed. Most germinate easily, and all grow quickly. Seeds are available from local garden centers or from seed catalogs. Many varieties—often the most popular and attractive ones—are available as bedding plants. Annuals are especially suited to mixing in a container, and a variety of annuals can be arranged in a single pot. Begin with a favorite flower, then add two or three other annuals to set it off or contrast with it. When you create a combination you particularly like, make a note of it so you can repeat it in the future.

Ageratum houstonianum

Ageratum, flossflower

Most modern cultivars are low-growing (4- to 12-inch), mounding plants. They produce dense clusters of fuzzy flowers in blue, pink, and white from summer through fall. Sow indoors 6 to 8 weeks before the last frost. Cover the seeds only lightly since they need light to germinate. Give them full sun to partial shade. Tuck in among other plants or plant 3 or 4 in a shallow container. They make a delightful combination with marigolds or pink petunias.

Antirrhinum majus

Snapdragon

The ever-popular snapdragon has a host of varieties adapted to container culture, mostly among the dwarf strains. The color range is vast: maroon, red, pink, white, lavender, and yellow. Some snapdragons have the typical "dragon's mouth" flower so fascinating to children, while others have double flowers, and still others, open blooms. Sow indoors 6 to 8 weeks before the last frost. In moderate climates, sow in late summer for winter bloom. Place containers in full sun. Remove faded flower spikes for continuous bloom. Snapdragons sometimes survive the winter to bloom for a second season. Cover the seeds only lightly since they need light to germinate. Dwarf forms, 7 to 15 inches high, make quite a show in planters.

Asparagus densiflorus

Asparagus fern

This is not a true fern, but an ornamental asparagus that forms an attractive, fluffy mass of green foliage. Seedlings grow very slowly, so it is best purchased as a transplant. Use in full sun and partial shade. Bring indoors over the winter to reuse the following year. 'Sprengeri' produces open, airy foliage on long, trailing branches and is ideal for hanging baskets. The white flowers are insignificant but produce long-lasting red berries. 'Meyersii' produces upright, foxtail stems perfect as a focal planting or green background.

Begonia semperflorens-cultorum hybrids

Wax begonia, fibrous begonia

Among the most popular of all annuals, wax begonias do equally well in sun or shade. Choose from varieties with white, pink, rose, or red flowers and green or bronze foliage. These begonias form compact mounds, 6 to 12 inches in height, covered in flowers from summer through fall. Although you can sow them indoors 12 to 14 weeks before the last frost (without covering the seeds, since they need light to germinate), these slow-to-mature plants are best bought in trays at planting-out time. Use alone or in combination in planters and baskets of all sorts. Bring plants or cuttings inside for winter bloom on a bright windowsill.

Brassica oleracea acephala

Flowering kale, ornamental cabbage

Grown for their strikingly colored foliage in white, pink, red, magenta, and purple, these plants form rounded or ruffled, roselike heads, 12 to 15 inches across, that take on their full color in cool weather and remain attractive for more than a month. Start indoors 6 to 8 weeks before planting out. Grow in full sun. For early summer color in warm climates, start in late winter. In cool climates, start in spring for fall color. This annual looks especially good as a specimen plant in its own container.

Begonia semperflorens-cultorum

Browallia speciosa

Browallia speciosa

Browallia, amethyst flower

Relatively unknown, browallia makes a charming annual for hanging baskets, with its numerous lavender, blue, or white flowers. It has trailing to semi-upright stems 8 to 18 inches long, depending on the cultivar. It does well in sun or shade and is easy to grow, flowering from summer to fall. Sow indoors 6 to 8 weeks before the last frost. Do not cover the seeds as they need light to germinate. Browallia is an excellent cut flower. Cut back and bring inside in fall for winter bloom.

Calendula officinalis

Calendula, pot marigold

The bright, daisylike, single or double flowers of the calendula are edible and often used in soups and stews. They come in yellow and orange shades as well as ivory, sometimes with a dark center. Compact varieties 10 to 18 inches in height are best for containers. Sow them indoors 4 to 6 weeks before the desired planting date or directly outdoors in sun or partial shade. Start this cool-season plant in the fall in warm climates for

late winter bloom or in early spring in cold climates for summer bloom. Calendula looks good alone or in mixtures in pots, tubs, and planters, and will take sharp frosts.

Campanula isophylla

Italian bellflower

The bell-shaped flowers in blue or white on 18- to 24-inch trailing stems are charming in a hanging basket. Buy young plants in the spring for summer bloom as seeds are rarely available. Give full sun to partial shade. Prune back in fall and bring indoors or take cuttings.

Catharanthus rosea

Madagascar periwinkle

Bright, phloxlike flowers in red, pink, rose, and white, often with a contrasting center, stand out against glossy foliage in this popular annual. They bloom

from spring right through fall. There are both dwarf, shrubby types to 10 inches in height and low-growing (6-inch) trailing varieties that spread to 24 inches in length. Sow indoors 12 weeks before the last frost. This is one plant that does not balk at hot, humid summers: in fact, it performs poorly where summers are cool, and tolerates dry conditions. Full sun is best, although partial shade is acceptable. It is a perfect choice for sunny window boxes, pots, and hanging baskets.

Celosia argentea var. cristata

Celosia

There are two distinct types of celosia. The plume celosia (*C. cristata plumosa*) produces feathery flowers; the cockscomb celosia (*C. cristata childsii*) has curious flowers resembling a rooster's comb. Both offer brightly colored, long-lasting blooms in scarlet, yellow, pink, and purple. Their foliage runs from yellowish to green to deep red. They range in height from 6 to 36 inches, but dwarf varieties are best for containers. Sow outdoors after the soil warms or,

preferably, indoors 4 weeks earlier, barely covering the seed. Plant in full sun to partial shade. Celosia are most attractive in combination with other plants.

Centaurea cineraria

See *Senecio cineraria*

Centaurea cyanus

Bachelor's button, cornflower

The charming blue, violet, pink, red, or white buttonlike flowers of the dwarf selections of bachelor's button are borne singly on 10- to 15-inch stalks over silvery gray foliage. Look for heat-resistant varieties, as old-fashioned cultivars tend to stop blooming at the beginning of summer. Sow directly in place in early spring or indoors 4 weeks prior to setting out, and give full sun. Combine with other annuals in window boxes and planters. Bachelor's button makes a good cut flower.

Dahlia hybrid

Dianthus barbatus

Dahlia hybrids

Dahlia

Most dahlias are grown from tuberous roots, but a few of the dwarf types are commonly offered as annuals. They come in single, semidouble, or double forms and in a wide variety of colors including yellow, orange, pink, red, and white. Most seed-grown types produce compact plants less than 18 inches in height. Start seed indoors 4 to 6 weeks prior to the last frost, then plant in full sun; they'll bloom until frost. The container can be brought indoors in the fall, allowed to dry out, then stored in a cool, dry place over the winter, or the tuberous roots can be dug up and stored in sand, vermiculite, or peat moss. Dahlias are attractive both in combination with other plants and in individual pots.

Dianthus barbatus

Sweet william

The highly fragrant flowers of sweet william are borne in dense clusters over a basal mat of dark green foliage. Although the plants can measure up to 18 inches in height, dwarf varieties are much smaller—3 to 6 inches. The flowers come in red, rose-purple, white, and multicolors. Sow outdoors after the final spring frost or indoors 6 to 8 weeks earlier. It is preferable to purchase transplants, though, as some varieties are biennials and won't bloom until the second year. Give them full sun or partial shade. They are a good choice for mixed hanging basket plantings.

Dianthus chinensis

China pink

The lightly fragrant flowers of the China pink are frilly and lacy, as if trimmed by pinking shears. They are produced spring through fall on stiff, upright 9- to 18-inch stems over bluish, grasslike foliage. The color range includes white, pink, red, lilac, and bicolors. Remove faded flowers to stimulate further bloom. Sow outdoors after the final spring frost or indoors 6 to 8 weeks earlier. Give China pinks sun, with some afternoon shade in dry areas. They look good massed together in pots and also mixed with other annuals in window boxes.

Gazania rigens

Gazania

These large, brightly colored, daisylike flowers measure 4 to 5 inches across and come in shades of yellow, cream, orange, pink, bronze, and red, some with contrasting centers. They are borne over a long season on erect 8-inch stalks over a rosette of dandelionlike leaves with silvery undersides. Give them full sun, not only to increase the number of flowers, but to make sure they stay open for a long time, since they close when shaded (and at night and on cloudy days). Sow outdoors after all danger of frost has passed or indoors 4 to 6 weeks prior. They are very colorful in large pots and boxes.

Gerbera jamesonii

Gerbera, Transvaal daisy

The gerbera forms a massive rosette of green leaves and strong, straight flower stalks from 8 to 18 inches tall, depending on the cultivar. Each bears a single large long-lasting daisylike flower, single or double, in clear shades of white, pink, salmon, orange, or red. Sow indoors 14 to 18 weeks prior to setting out after the soil has warmed up, or buy plants in spring. Gerbera prefers full sun or partial shade. It is a showstopper in its own pot or combined with other plants in a larger planter, and makes an excellent cut flower. It will overwinter in areas where temperatures rarely drop much below freezing.

Iberis umbellata

Candytuft

Candytuft produces 6- to 15-inch mounds of green foliage covered with umbrella-shaped clusters of red, pink, lavender, purple, and white flowers. Sow outdoors after all danger of frost has passed or indoors 6 to 8 weeks earlier. Candytuft does best in full sun to partial shade and cool conditions. If it stops blooming in hot weather, prune it back. In hot climates, sow seed every 2 to 3 weeks for continuous bloom. Candytuft is a good choice for pots and window boxes. Dwarf varieties are attractive mixed with other flowers in hanging baskets.

Impatiens balsamina

Lobularia maritima

Impatiens balsamina

Balsam

The thick, watery, upright stems measure 10 to 12 inches high in dwarf cultivars. They support deep green leaves and flowers, usually double, in a wide range of colors, including white, pink, rose, scarlet, and purple. Look for cultivars that hold their flowers well above the leaves. Sow outdoors after all danger of frost has passed or indoors 6 to 8 weeks earlier. Balsam does best in partial shade, although full sun is fine in cool climates. It is most attractive in combination with other plants.

Impatiens hawkeri hybrids

New Guinea impatiens

This plant forms an upright, dense 12- to 24-inch mound of green to bronze foliage, usually highlighted by colorful markings in white, yellow, cream, pink, or red. The extralarge flowers in tones of red, orange, pink, lavender, or purple are often brilliant. Since the most highly colored cultivars do not reproduce true

from seed, purchase transplants in spring after the soil has warmed up. New Guinea impatiens can also be sown indoors 10 weeks before the last frost date. Unlike the more common garden impatiens (*I. walleriana*), New Guinea impatiens does best in full sun or only partial shade. It blooms the year around in frost-free climates; elsewhere, bring cuttings inside for the winter. New Guinea impatiens are spectacular in individual pots or in combination with other plants in large planters.

Impatiens walleriana

Impatiens, busy lizzie

Here is the star of the shaded container garden, producing masses of blooms over a long season in deeper shade than most other flowers accept. The mounding plants with watery stems range from 8 to 14 inches high, depending on the cultivar. They produce nonstop flat-faced flowers in red, pink, salmon, lavender, purple, and bicolors, either single or double, over green or bronze leaves. Sow indoors 10 weeks before all danger of frost has passed. Although

they do best in shade to partial shade, many modern cultivars are quite sun resistant. Impatiens wilt quickly at the slightest sign of drought: keep the soil evenly moist. Pinch as needed to maintain compactness. Impatiens can be maintained indoors over the winter for another season of bloom. This truly all-purpose container plant can be used in hanging baskets, single pots, mixed planters, hanging cylinders, and wall planters. They are at home everywhere.

Lobelia erinus

Lobelia

Immensely popular in container gardens and for good reason, lobelias bloom abundantly over a long season. Their tiny flowers are in shades of lavender, pink, and white, but blue is especially popular. They're borne on erect or trailing plants, depending on the cultivar, over fine green to bronze foliage. Sow indoors 12 weeks before final frost or buy transplants in spring, and give full sun or partial shade. If the

plant loses steam in midsummer, prune back to stimulate new growth and bloom. Trailing varieties are ideal for mixed hanging baskets and tubs, and also as ground covers for trees and shrubs, as their cascading habit hides harsh container edges. Erect types look wonderful in mixed tub plantings and also make good cut flowers.

Lobularia maritima

Sweet alyssum

This low-growing (2- to 8-inch) mounding or trailing plant produces dense clusters of tiny perfumed flowers in mauve, rose, lavender, purple, and white. Sow outdoors in early spring or indoors 4 to 6 weeks before the last frost. Do not cover the seeds as they need light to germinate. Give sweet alyssum full sun to partial shade. It looks best combined with other flowers, especially in hanging baskets. Use also as a ground cover for trees and shrubs in containers. If its flowering diminishes (and it is likely to do so in hot weather), prune back to stimulate renewed bloom.

Pelargonium peltatum

Portulaca grandiflora

Nemesia strumosa

Nemesia

The pouched flowers of nemesia come in just about every color but green, on dense, compact plants ranging from 8 to 24 inches high. Sow indoors 4 to 6 weeks before planting out or directly outdoors after all danger of frost has passed. Nemesia does best in full sun and cool conditions, and is not a good choice for areas with hot summers. Pinch regularly to stimulate compact growth and heavy bloom. It is charming in mixed basket plantings, pots, and window boxes. Dwarf types are best for containers.

Nicotiana alata

Nicotiana, flowering tobacco

Dwarf types of nicotiana are available in a wide range of colors, including red, rose, lavender, white, and lime green. The tubular flowers, sometimes perfumed, are borne on slender stems above low-growing rosettes from summer to fall. Sow indoors 6 to 8 weeks before planting out or directly outdoors after all danger of frost has passed. Does best in afternoon

shade in hot areas. Makes an excellent choice for individual pots as well as mixed tub plantings. Good cut flower.

Nierembergia hippomanica

Nierembergia

This annual forms a dense, neat mat of fine-textured foliage covered in cup-shaped blooms from summer through fall. Blue, purple, and white varieties are available. Sow indoors 10 to 12 weeks before planting out. It does best in afternoon shade in hot areas, and may overwinter in mild climates. Nierembergia is ideal for pots, window boxes, and hanging baskets. It is a good replacement for trailing lobelia in hot summer areas where the latter tends to die back.

Pelargonium × hortorum

Zonal geranium

Among the most popular container plants, zonal geraniums bloom spring through fall— even through the winter if brought inside. They produce large rounded clusters of single or double flowers in white, pink,

rose, red, scarlet, and salmon. The scallop-shaped leaves are often marked with a distinctive brown horseshoe. Zonal geraniums can be grown from seed sown indoors 12 to 16 weeks prior to planting out, and also by cuttings taken at any time. Variegated leaf varieties—with leaves striped and blotched with white, pink, cream, or yellow—are also popular, but can be reproduced only by cuttings. Zonal geraniums can easily be kept under 24 inches by pinching regularly. Bring them inside in fall for winter bloom.

Pelargonium peltatum

Ivy geranium

A very popular plant for hanging baskets, the ivy geranium produces long, trailing stems to 36 inches and ivylike leaves. The flowers, in shades of white, lavender, pink, and red, often with dark markings, are borne in clusters. Although they can be sown indoors 16 to 18 weeks prior to planting out, growing from seed is time-consuming and the plants are rarely as interesting as those produced by cuttings. It is easiest simply to

buy ready-made hanging baskets in the spring. Although it likes sunny locations, the ivy geranium will bloom better if given a bit of afternoon shade in hot climates. Take cuttings or bring baskets indoors in the fall.

Petunia hybrids

Petunia

Who doesn't recognize the petunia in spite of its numerous disguises? Single or double flowered, ruffled or plain edged, large or small flowered, in all shades of white, pink, salmon, red, violet, blue, purple, and even yellow—there is almost no limit to the possibilities. Grandiflora varieties produce the largest, most colorful flowers, but are not as vigorous or floriferous as the multiflora varieties, which have smaller blooms. Petunias form bushy 12 to 15-inch mounds, and some types cascade nicely. Sow indoors 10 to 12 weeks before final frost or buy transplants. Pinch occasionally to increase flowering. Give full sun. This multipurpose plant works well in tubs, hanging baskets, window boxes, and mixed plantings of all kinds.

Primula obconica

Schizanthus × wisetonensis

A strain of trailing petunias with very long stems, going by the name of perennial petunia or ground cover petunia, or by the trade names 'Surfinia' or 'Superpetunia', is becoming increasingly popular. It bears very small but numerous flowers throughout the season and overwinters in moderate climates.

Phlox drummondii
Annual phlox

Dense bunches of blue, violet, crimson, pink, yellow, and white rounded to star-shaped flowers, often in bicolor combinations, characterize this popular annual. Dwarf, bushy types, to about 7 inches, are better for containers than the erect varieties. Since annual phlox resents transplanting, either sow directly outdoors after all danger of frost has passed or sow indoors in peat pots 4 to 6 weeks before planting out. Don't thin out the weakest seedlings, as they often offer the best color. Give full sun. Annual phlox blooms summer and fall in cool climates, but slows down during the hottest part of summer elsewhere. Grow in pots and hanging baskets.

Portulaca grandiflora
Portulaca

This is the ideal choice for hot, dry sites and poor soils where other annuals wither away, but full sun is a must. Portulaca also tolerates shallow soils, making it the perfect selection for small planting pockets in nonstandard containers. It produces single or double roselike flowers with a satiny sheen in shades of red, pink, rose, lavender, yellow, and white, often with a contrasting yellow center. The semitrailing stems produce fleshy, succulent leaves. Unlike old-fashioned types, modern hybrids stay open all day. Sow directly outdoors after all danger of frost has passed or indoors 4 to 6 weeks ahead. Grow in pots and hanging baskets.

Primula
Primrose

There are three types of primrose commonly grown as annuals. Fairy primrose (*P. malacoides*) is a spring bloomer in warm climates and a summer bloomer in cooler ones. It produces a flat rosette of oblong leaves and 4- to 18-inch stalks with whorls of white, pink, rose, red, or lavender flowers. German primrose (*P. obconica*) has a similar blooming period but differs by its rounded leaves and single cluster of white, pink, lavender, and purple flowers. Both act as short-lived perennials in mild climates. The polyantha primrose (*P. × polyantha*) is a more brightly colored spring bloomer. See Perennials and Biennials on pages 73 and 74 for more information on this hardier form. Primroses are difficult to grow from seed at home and are best purchased as transplants. Give them shade to partial shade and cool conditions. They are good for pots and hanging baskets.

Salvia splendens
Salvia, scarlet sage

Its bright colors and long blooming period make this annual very popular. Dwarf cultivars—the ones most suited to container culture—reach about 12 inches in height, producing a long-lasting spike of tubular flowers over dense, dark green foliage. Salvia is best known for its bright scarlet red coloration. There are also white, pink, purple, and blue selections. Sow indoors 6 to 8 weeks prior to the final frost without covering the seeds as they need light to germinate. Give full sun or partial shade. Grow in large pots and boxes. Cool down its strong hues with white petunias. Hummingbirds love them.

Schizanthus × wisetonensis
Butterfly flower, poor-man's-orchid

Both common names for this plant are quite appropriate, for the numerous flowers look like little butterflies hovering over the delicate, lacy foliage, and in multicolor combinations of pink, yellow, violet, orange, red, and magenta, they are as colorful as any orchid. They are 12 to 24 inches high. Sow indoors 12 weeks before the last frost. Don't cover the fine seeds, but place the seed tray in darkness until germination occurs. Full sun gives best bloom, but partial shade may be the only way to keep this annual, adapted to coastal areas, cool. Plant in relatively small pots, as it blooms

Tagetes erecta × patula

Torenia fournieri

best when its roots are con-
stricted. A good basket and tub
plant, it blooms late, which
makes it an ideal substitute for
early blooming annuals once
they have weakened.

Senecio cineraria

Dusty-miller

This delightful accent plant
is not grown for its infrequent
daisylike blooms, but for its
deeply divided, woolly white foliage. It adds a silvery sheen
to mixed plantings, helping to
bring out the colors of the other
flowers in the container or
soften contrasts between overly
divergent hues. Modern cultivars are dense and compact and
need little pinching except to
remove the flowers that add
nothing to the plant's appearance. Sow indoors 8 to 10 weeks
before the last frost. Give full
sun or partial shade. Although
treated as an annual, dusty-
miller often survives the winter.
If so, prune it back harshly to
maintain its compact growth.
Centaurea cineraria, also
called dusty-miller, is a similar
plant and requires the same
treatment.

Solenostemon scutellariodes

Coleus

This fast-growing plant is popular for its spectacularly multicolored leaves in white, pink,
yellow, red, purple, cream, and
green. The leaves also vary in
shape from heart-shaped to
fringed or lancelike. The blue
flowers are insignificant and
should be pinched out when
seen. Sow indoors 6 to 8 weeks
before the soil warms up after
the last frost. Don't cover the
seeds, as they need light to germinate. Plant outdoors in shade
to partial shade. Pinch taller
varieties to produce denser
growth. Coleus looks good in
pots and tubs; trailing varieties
are available for hanging baskets. Take cuttings of favorite
colors for indoor use over
winter.

Tagetes

Marigold

This popular, easy-to-grow container plant is offered in three
major types. African marigolds
(*T. erecta*) are generally tall-
growing plants, 2 to 3 feet tall,
although dwarf forms (12 inches) are available. They are easily

distinguished by their huge,
fully double flowers in yellow,
orange, or off-white. French
marigolds (*T. patula*) are shorter (7 to 12 inches) and bear
much smaller but more numerous flowers. They may be yellow,
orange, bronze, or russet, and
single, double, or semidouble in
form. Many are bicolored or
striped. Triploid marigolds (*T.
erecta × patula*) result from a
cross between the two previous
plants, but generally resemble
the African marigold in form
and color. Triploids, which are
sterile, do not put energy into
seed production, so are particularly floriferous. All three can
be sown indoors 4 to 6 weeks
prior to the last frost date.
French marigolds can also be
sown directly in place. Give
them full sun. All marigolds are
attractive in mixed plantings in
tubs and window boxes. French
marigolds are also choice in
mixed hanging baskets.

Thunbergia alata

Black-eyed-susan vine

This delightful climbing plant
has orange, yellow, or white
blooms, mostly with dark centers. It twines up trellises and

other supports to more than 6
feet in height, hiding them with
dense, ivylike foliage, but also
can be allowed to trail gracefully from tubs, window boxes, or
hanging baskets. Sow indoors 6
to 8 weeks before the last frost
or outdoors when the soil warms
up. Give it full sun to partial
shade. It prefers cool summers
and will overwinter in mild climates. Elsewhere, bring inside
in fall for use as a flowering
winter houseplant.

Torenia fournieri

Wishbone flower

This clump-forming annual
bears curious flowers somewhat
like those of the snapdragon,
but with a wishbonelike structure in the center. The flowers
are always multicolored, some
in shades of purple and lavender, others in pink and red, with
a yellow or white mark on the
lower lobe. The plant grows 10
to 12 inches tall. Sow indoors
10 to 12 weeks before the last
frost. Do not cover the seeds
since they need light to germinate. Give partial to deep shade.
Wishbone flower is ideal for
pots, tubs, or window boxes in
cool, humid spots.

Verbena hybrid

Viola × wittrockiana

Tropaeolum majus

Nasturtium

The bright orange, yellow, pink, red, and white flowers of the nasturtium, often bicolored, recall the gardens of yesteryear. Some are quite fragrant. Look for varieties whose blooms are held well above the rounded leaves. The foliage, flowers, and seeds are all edible, adding a peppery tang to salads. Sow outdoors after all danger of frost has passed. Nasturtium does best in full sun and cool conditions. Climbing types are spectacular when trained up a trellis or other support or allowed to dangle from hanging baskets. The bushy growth of dwarf hybrids (12 to 15 inches in height) is ideal for mixed tub plantings.

Verbena hybrids

Verbena

Particularly brilliant red, pink, blue, purple, and white flowers, often with a white eye, are borne in profusion in terminal clusters over aromatic green or grayish foliage. Choose among trailing, bushy, or erect cultivars. Sow indoors 12 to 14 weeks before the last frost. Do not cover the fine seeds, but place in darkness until they germinate. Even better, buy transplants, as verbenas are not the easiest plants to grow from seed. For best results, give them full sun and dry conditions. They bloom well even in the heat of summer. Verbenas stand out in pots, window boxes, and hanging baskets.

Vinca major 'Variegata'

Variegated periwinkle

Although hardy to Zone 7, this plant is so commonly grown as a cascading summer window box plant that it is more suitable to treat it here than as a perennial. It bears sporadic, pale blue flowers, but the shiny white and green leaves and long trailing branches, are so attractive that one may not even notice the blooms. Start from cuttings in late winter or early spring. Variegated periwinkle grows equally well in sun or shade. The all-green version is also cultivated in containers, as is the hardier dwarf periwinkle (*Vinca minor*). All are perfect choices for softening harsh edges of hanging baskets, tubs, and window boxes.

Viola × wittrockiana

Pansy

This popular low-growing annual (actually a short-lived perennial) is grown as a winter bloomer in warm climates and as an early-spring bloomer in climates with hot summers. Only in climates with cool summers does it really bloom from spring through fall, although modern hybrids are increasingly heat resistant. The flat, broad flowers come in white, pink, purple, yellow, blue, red, orange, and bronze, and often feature blotches of a contrasting color, looking a bit like a smiling face. Although they can be sown indoors 10 to 12 weeks before planting out, the seedlings need cool growing conditions, so most people prefer to buy transplants. Plant them as soon as the ground can be worked to take full advantage of their early blooms. Give full sun. This very versatile plant can be used in pots, tubs, window boxes, and hanging baskets.

Small-flowered "pansies" are known as violas. They come from a wide variety of species, including the horned viola (*V. cornuta*), the johnny-jump-up (*V. tricolor*), and hybrids between these and garden pansies. Their numerous but tiny flowers make for a charming display in mixed plantings. They are generally short-lived perennials but are usually treated as annuals when grown in containers.

Zinnia elegans

Zinnia

This is an easy, all-purpose, fast-growing annual offering dwarf, intermediate, and tall growth habits. Its flowers come in a wide range of forms— single, semidouble, and double, and button shaped, dahlialike, and cactus flowered, just to name a few—and nearly every color of the rainbow, plus bicolors. Sow directly outdoors after the last frost or indoors 4 weeks beforehand. Lightly cover seed. Tall varieties can be massed in large containers for showy display and cut flowers. Shorter, bushier varieties are excellent for potted color in full sun and hot conditions.

Aster × frikartii

Chrysanthemum hybrids

PERENNIAL AND BIENNIAL FLOWERS

Both perennials and biennials are available ready to bloom or already blooming from nurseries. Not only do these plants give you instant satisfaction, but you can see exactly what you're getting, both in plant shape and in flower. Most nurseries sell plants that are well started from seeds or cuttings, but which are still quite small. Some species bloom the first year, but many take up to three years to reach their full potential. Biennials, of course, always bloom the second year from seed. Most biennials bloom in early spring, then die after blooming. The selection in most local garden centers is limited. The next best way to purchase perennials is as mail-order plants.

Armeria maritima
Sea-pink, sea-thrift

Perennial. The sea-pink forms a dense cushion of grasslike foliage that is attractive even when the plant is not in bloom. Heads of pink, rose, or white flowers rise from 6- to 12-inch stalks in May and June and sporadically throughout the year in mild climates. The mound slowly expands over a several-year period to cover 1 to 1½ feet in diameter. When the center begins to die out, it is time to divide. Plant in a well-drained soil in full sun. Sea-pink, as the name suggests, was originally a seaside plant and is very tolerant of salt spray. Use in pots as well as planters of low-growing plants. Hardy to Zone 4.

Aster species
Hardy aster

Perennial. Asters are daisylike plants offered in a variety of shades, mostly whites, pinks, and purples. Most are late summer to fall bloomers. Among the wide range of asters, the best choices for containers are the dwarf types. Plant in full sun in a relatively moist soil. Due to their rapid growth, they need division every two years, and sometimes even annually. The following types are popular.

A. × frikartii. Lavender-blue flowers appear as early as June and continue until October, making this the longest flowering of the asters. Height reaches: 2½ feet. This is one perennial that does especially well in warm climates. Hardy to Zone 6 (Zone 5 with a protective mulch).

A. novi-belgii (michaelmas-daisy). This group of typical "fall asters" begins blooming in August and continues for well over a month. Dwarf hybrids as short as 12 to 15 inches are available in a wide range of colors. Most of these are actually crosses between *A. novi-belgii* and *A. dumosus.* Hardy to Zone 4.

Note that the popular China aster (*Callistephus*), an annual, is not a true aster, nor even a close relative.

Aurinia saxatilis
Basket-of-gold

Perennial. Basket-of-gold has grayish foliage and grows 6 to 12 inches high. Clusters of golden yellow flowers cover the plant in early to mid-spring. Cut stems back by one third after blooming to increase its life expectancy. It is most easily reproduced by cuttings and does best in full sun in a well-drained soil. Hot, humid summer weather can be fatal. It is a top choice for hanging baskets and edging. Hardy to Zone 4.

Campanula species
Bellflower

This genus offers a wide range of plants, mostly with blue or white bell-shaped flowers, that are well suited to container conditions. Most are easy to grow under sunny to partially shady conditions and with ordinary soil mix. Bellflowers require only infrequent division. The dwarf or rock garden types are especially charming in hanging baskets and pots.

C. carpatica (Carpathian harebell). Perennial. This delightful mounded plant 6 to 12 inches high produces blue, purple, or white flowers for a long period, June to August. Hardy to Zone 4.

Coreopsis with *Vinca*

Delphinium hybrids

C. medium (Canterbury bells). Biennial. Large bell-shaped flowers in blue, white, purple, or pink are produced from June to August on sturdy, upright stalks growing 2 to 3 feet. Cup and saucer (*C. medium* 'Calycanthema') is a selection with a saucer-shaped calyx the same color as the flower. Hardy to Zone 4.

C. portenschlagiana (Dalmatian bellflower). Perennial. This mat-forming plant grows to 8 inches high and bears bluish purple flowers in June and July. Hardy to Zone 5.

C. poscharskyana (Serbian bellflower). Perennial. A sprawling plant cascades to 24 inches but is only 2 to 3 inches high. It bears numerous lilac flowers in June and July, and is quite drought resistant. Hardy to Zone 4.

Chrysanthemum hybrids

Chrysanthemum

Perennial. The genus *Chrysanthemum* has been broken up into several separate genera, leaving only a very few true chrysanthemums, none of them commonly cultivated. Most of the plants generally considered "mums" are now in the genus *Dendranthema*. However, for convenience's sake, they have been placed here. They are fall-flowering plants with daisylike or pompon flowers in every shade but blue. Cushion mums, with their dense low growth (they rarely exceed 15 inches) and numerous fall flowers, are among the best mums for containers. Supply them with full sun or partial shade and rich, evenly moist soil. Pinch regularly spring through midsummer to create a compact plant that will bear many flowers come fall. Divide annually to extend their notoriously short life. A tub dripping with cushion mums is a sight for sore eyes. Hardy to Zone 6 (Zone 5 with protection).

Coreopsis species and hybrids

Coreopsis

Perennial. The bright, sunny, daisylike flowers bloom much of the summer. They are generally in shades of yellow, but certain species offer pink or mahogany blooms. Any well-drained soil in full sun will do. Remove faded blooms to prolong flowering. This plant rarely needs division.

C. lanceolata (lance coreopsis). This is the most typical species, with lance-shaped leaves, as the name suggests. Flowers are yellow and may be single or double. Look for dwarf varieties of this otherwise tall plant. 'Baby Sun', for example, is only 18 to 20 inches tall, and 'Goldfink' is even smaller, at 10 to 12 inches. All bloom from July to September and make good cut flowers. Some lance coreopsis selections reproduce quite true from seed. Zone 4.

C. verticillata (threadleaf coreopsis). Very fine, lacy leaves characterize this plant, which is drought tolerant. Flowers are yellow. 'Moonbeam' (18 to 24 inches), with pale yellow flowers, and 'Zagreb' (12 inches), with golden yellow flowers, are choice cultivars that bloom from June to September. Zone 4.

Delphinium hybrids

Delphinium

Perennial. The towering spikes of the most popular delphiniums are typical features of the mixed border, but they're a bit tall for most containers. Intermediate (2 to 3 feet) and dwarf hybrids (less than 2 feet) seem better proportioned in pots. Flowers are white, pink, blue, lavender, violet, or purple, often with a dark or white eye called a "bee." Delphiniums bloom in early to mid-summer and may rebloom if the first flower stalk is cut off when it fades. Delphiniums are best reproduced by seed, as division is a delicate task. Full sun and moist, well-drained soil are ideal. Stake to protect from strong winds. This is a good specimen plant for pots or large tubs. In warm climates, it can be grown as an annual. Hardy to Zone 4.

Dianthus plumarius

Cottage-pink, grass-pink, Scotch-pink

Perennial. Cottage-pinks produce great quantities of rose, pink, red, or white blossoms in May and June, some 4 inches taller than the tufted, compact plants of about 8 inches. The gray-green leaves often persist through winter. The fringed,

Dicentra formosa

Papaver orientale

lacy flowers are about 1½ inches wide and can be solid or bicolored, single or double. Supply full sun and add limestone to the soil mix to make it slightly alkaline. Prune flowers after blooming so they won't go to seed. Cottage-pink makes a versatile container plant. Hardy to Zone 4. Other species of *Dianthus* are included on page 64.

Dicentra spectabilis

Bleeding-heart

Perennial. This old-fashioned garden plant has made quite a comeback and no wonder: Its arching flower stalks of pink, heart-shaped flowers are charming. The plant forms dense clumps 30 inches tall and 36 inches wide, with flower stalks held among and above the foliage. The attractive, deeply cut, bluish green leaves have the good sense to die back after the plant blooms in April and May, leaving space in the container garden for later blooming plants. Grow in partial shade and rich soil. Divide as necessary in spring or fall. 'Alba' has white flowers. Zone 3.

Hybrids of *D. eximia* and *D. formosa*, such as 'Luxuriant' and 'Bountiful', are also good container plants. They are only 12 to 18 inches high and bloom in shades of pink to red throughout the entire summer. Zone 4.

Geranium sanguineum

Bloodred geranium

Perennial. Don't confuse this plant with the zonal geranium and other tender kinds: the latter are actually in the genus *Pelargonium*, only a far-distant cousin. Bloodred geranium (so called because its leaves turn red in the fall) is a true geranium, a member of *Geranium*, a genus of hardy plants offering plenty of choice perennials for container gardens. It forms a 6- to 12-inch clump of deeply cut leaves, spreading to 2 feet in diameter. The flowers—magenta in the species, and pink to white, often with contrasting veins, in the cultivars—are produced copiously in spring and early summer. Give it full sun or partial shade and good drainage. Other hardy geraniums, most somewhat larger, also make choice container plants,

including *G. endressii*, with blue flowers; *G. endressii* 'Wargrave Pink', with clear pink flowers, and *G. himalayense*, with blue, purple, or lavender flowers. All are hardy to Zone 4.

Geum hybrids

Geum, avens

Perennial. The bright orange, red, or yellow single, double, or semidouble flowers of hybrid geums are borne on 24- to 30-inch branching stems over a dense basal cluster of toothed green leaves. If faded flowers are removed as they appear, geums will bloom throughout much of the summer. They prefer sun or partial shade and a well-drained location. Wet soil in winter, especially, can kill them. Dividing them regularly helps extend their longevity. They succeed best in areas with cool summers. Zone 6.

Heuchera sanguinea

Coralbells

Perennial. If coralbells didn't bloom, it probably would still be grown for its attractive, rounded, evergreen rosette of maple-

like leaves, often marked with silver. The leaves also take on a reddish cast in the fall, which lasts much of the winter. Coralbells does bloom, however, and its tiny but numerous pink bell-shaped flowers are carried on 1- to 2-foot wiry stems over much of the summer, especially if faded flower stalks are removed promptly. It prefers sun or partial shade and a well-drained but moist location. Divide every 3 years or so when the center of the plant becomes woody. It's a good accent plant for tubs and planters. Selected cultivars have more colorful leaves and flowers ranging from white to deep red. Zone 4.

Hylotelephium spectabile

Showy stonecrop

Perennial (previously known as *Sedum spectabile*). This mounded 2-foot plant with fleshy, light green leaves attracts butterflies. It flowers from August to frost, producing flat-topped clusters in pink, rose, or white. The flowers dry to a pleasing reddish brown and often last the winter. A very easy-to-grow plant, it tolerates both full sun and light

Phlox paniculata

Primula × polyantha

shade, and just about any kind of soil as long as it drains well. Once planted, showy stonecrop will take care of itself, so it is ideal for containers that are out of convenient reach. It is easily reproduced by division or stem cuttings. Zone 4.

Papaver orientale

Oriental poppy

Perennial. The huge 4- to 6-inch crepe-paper flowers of this June-blooming plant come in striking colors such as fire-engine red, burning orange, and luscious peach. Even the white-flowered forms are dramatic, for the flower usually has a black center and striking black blotches at the base of the petals. Each thick stem supports one giant flower. The grayish, toothed leaves disappear after flowering, leaving space for other plantings. Established plants resent being disturbed, so divide only when more plants are needed and then only when the plant is dormant, in August or early September. Give the

Oriental poppy full sun to partial shade and good drainage. The brilliant flowers are so dominant that it is best to plant with late-blooming perennials so there is no competition. Zone 4.

Penstemon gloxinioides

Gloxinia penstemon, beardtongue

Perennial. The red, pink, lavender, or white tubular flowers of the beardtongue are borne on slender stems up to 2 feet tall. They appear in June and July, with good repeat bloom if the old flower stalks are removed. Rather tender, this plant does best on the West Coast, although it can be grown elsewhere if well protected during the winter. Give it full sun to light shade and a well-drained, gritty soil to prevent any accumulation of water at the roots in winter. This plant is especially popular in containers, partly because it is easier to meet its special demands in a pot than in a garden. Start new plants from cuttings of basal shoots, as it is hard to divide. There are many other

kinds of penstemon, some of which are better adapted to cooler climates. Zone 7.

Phlox paniculata

Summer phlox, garden phlox

Perennial. This popular summer bloomer is even more attractive grown in containers than in the garden—and that's saying a lot. The flower heads are conical and composed of dozens of flat-faced tubular flowers in various shades of white, pink, red, and violet, often with a contrasting eye. The sturdy stems are well clothed in dark green leaves. Pruning out faded flower stalks will often keep summer phlox blooming until fall. Watch out for powdery mildew, which causes severe leaf loss, although apparently no permanent damage. It can be prevented by spraying the leaves with a fungicide or a liquid antitranspirant (normally used for spraying evergreens in late fall). Summer phlox prefers sun or partial shade and a moist, well-drained location. Divide every three years or so. It is a striking accent plant for tubs and planters. Zone 4.

Primula species

Primrose

Perennial. The very name *primula* means "spring," and these plants, along with the bulbs, have come to symbolize the coming of a new growing season. There are literally hundreds of species of primrose and thousands of cultivars. All are spring-blooming plants, and most are rather low-growing plants, often with tongue-shaped leaves growing from a ground-hugging rosette. Some have upright stalks bearing rounded clusters of flowers; others have flower stalks so short that the flowers seem to grow right out of the ground. Primroses are intolerant of hot, dry weather; move the containers to a cool, shady spot after they finish blooming. Divide frequently to maintain vigor.

P. japonica (Japanese primrose). One of the taller species, it reaches 2 feet in height, each stem bearing several tiers of flowers in red, white, pink, or crimson. It prefers very moist—even boggy—conditions. Zone 5.

Stachys byzantina

Anemone blanda

P. ✕ polyantha (polyantha primrose). This very complex hybrid group includes many different species in its background. As a result, polyantha primroses can look very different from each other, ranging from ground-hugging dwarfs to 1-foot "giants." The colors range over about every shade possible, including green, and many flowers have large rings of contrasting colors around their centers. The hardiness of polyantha primrose is highly variable, but some survive into Zone 3.

P. vulgaris (English primrose). This is one of the many parents of the polyantha primrose, and the two are often confused. It bears solitary or numerous flowers on 6-inch stems. They are pale yellow in the species, but myriad colors in the hybrids. Zone 5.

Primrose species usually treated as annuals are described on page 67.

Salvia nemorosa hybrids

Perennial salvia

Perennial. Gray-green foliage and spikes of violet to deep pink flowers characterize this group of plants. They are actually a complex group of hybrids based on *S. nemorosa* but also involving other species. You may find some of them listed as *S. ✕ superba* or *S. ✕ sylvestris*. All are easy to grow and bloom all summer. Give them full sun and well-drained soil. They multiply by cuttings or division. Some winter protection is needed in cold climates. They are among the rare hardy perennials that do very well in warm climates, and are versatile plants that can be used in tubs and pots. Zone 4.

Stachys byzantina

Lamb's-ears, woolly betony

Perennial. This plant is grown for its foliage alone. The soft, silky leaves—a true pleasure to stroke—indeed feel just like a lamb's ears. The leaves are so covered in long white hair that they show almost no green. Most gardeners remove the spikes of pinkish purple flowers to enhance the silvery effect of the

foliage. The cultivar 'Silver Carpet' goes one better, as it does not flower. Give lamb's-ears full sun and well-drained soil. Divide every 4 years or so. The soft white foliage adds permanent color to window boxes and planters and helps highlight the blooms of other plants. Zone 4.

Stokesia laevis

Stokes' aster

Perennial. The flowers of this plant, solitary and up to 4 inches across, look much like giant bachelor's-buttons. They are produced in July and August on 1- to 1½-foot stalks and come in shades of blue, lavender, and occasionally white. The dark green lance-shaped leaves are mostly grouped at the base of the plant. Give the plant full sun and very well-drained soil, or it will tend to rot during winter. Divide every 4 years or so. Winter protection is needed in cold climates. It is a good choice for mixed planters. Zone 6.

HARDY BULBS

Hardy bulbs come from cool to cold climate areas; most will only bloom and grow normally if they undergo a long period of cold temperatures, equivalent to a normal winter. This group includes crocus, tulips, narcissus, and most other spring bloomers. All hardy bulbs, except some lilies, are sold exclusively for fall planting. They are available in garden centers from late summer into winter.

Allium

Flowering onion

There are many species of flowering onions. They range from only a few inches in height to 5 feet. Most produce dense clusters of flowers in shades of purple, violet, magenta, or blue, although some have white or yellow blooms. Don't worry about any oniony scent in these kissing cousins to onions and garlic: most allium flowers are odorless, and some are even beautifully perfumed. Small species such as *A. neapolitanum*—which produces 12- to 18-inch stems of perfumed white flowers—are the best choices for container growing. Flowering

Crocus species

Lilium species

onions offer a long blooming season in late spring to early summer. Give sun or light shade.

Anemone blanda

Anemone, windflower

This tiny plant bears bright, starlike flowers in blue, purple, rose, or white with a contrasting yellow center and sometimes a white halo. It grows only 4 to 6 inches high and is a very early bloomer. Soak the tiny black tubers overnight before planting. It is hard to tell which side is up, so if in doubt, plant the bulb on its side. Give sun or light shade.

Convallaria majalis

Lily-of-the-valley

This old-fashioned, highly perfumed flower does especially well in containers. It produces 6- to 8-inch stalks of bell-shaped white or pink flowers in midspring. The broad, dark green leaves may begin to look tired by midsummer. If so, clip them off. Hardy to Zone 3, lily-of-the-valley does not need special care: just pot it in the fall and leave the container outdoors to undergo local winter conditions.

It will bloom on its own come spring. It prefers shadier, more humid conditions than most bulbs; do not withhold water in summer. Give light to heavy shade.

Crocus

Crocus

Crocuses, among the first flowers to bloom in spring, produce stemless, cup-shaped flowers over a clump of grasslike leaves. Barely cover bulbs with soil mix. Dutch crocuses (*C. vernus*) reach 5 inches in height, with especially large flowers. The smaller *C. chrysanthus* blooms earlier and bears more flowers. Both come in shades of blue, purple, gold, and white, as well as bicolors. Flowers open fully only on sunny days. Give sun or light shade.

Galanthus nivalis

Snowdrop

This bulb vies with the winter aconite as the earliest spring bulb of all. It produces nodding white flowers with green-tipped

inner petals on arching 6-inch stems. The leaves are narrow and grasslike. 'Flore Pleno' has double flowers. Snowdrop prefers partial shade.

Hyacinthus orientalis

Dutch hyacinth

This popular container plant should always be placed where its perfume will be most appreciated: near a doorway, along a frequently used path, beneath an open window. The stiff 9-inch spikes are densely covered in star-shaped flowers in white, pink, rose, red, yellow, salmon, blue, or purple. Over the years, the bulb divides and produces longer, looser, arching stalks. Buy large bulbs for a more spectacular display. Give sun to partial shade.

Iris

Iris

The best-known irises are those, such as bearded iris and Siberian iris, with creeping rhizomes, but there are also several bulbous irises of interest. Two, *I. reticulata* and *I. danfordiae*, are miniatures no more than 6 inches high that bloom in late

winter or very early spring. They are spectacular in pots or bowls. *I. reticulata* is available in a wide range of shades of blue, violet, and purple, usually with distinct white or yellow patches. *I. danfordiae* is bright yellow. Dutch iris, a hybrid form based on *I. xiphium*, is much taller— 10 to 24 inches—and comes in blue, purple, yellow, orange, or white. Not very hardy, it needs ample protection in cold areas. It can also be stored, dry, in the refrigerator over the winter for planting outdoors in early spring. It blooms later than its miniature counterparts, at about midspring. Both types do best in sun or partial shade.

Lilium

Lily

Lilies are very popular in outdoor gardens and also in pots. The strongly upright stems are cloaked in arching lance-shaped leaves and are capped by clusters of often large flowers. They come in all sizes, from dwarf and intermediate types (the

Tulipa species

Agapanthus species

best ones for containers) to giants more than 6 feet tall. Forms include pendulous Turk's-caps and upright or outward-facing trumpet shapes. Many are perfumed. All colors, from white to pink, orange, deep red, and purple are possible, often with markings and shadings of distinctly different colors. Asiatic hybrids are very popular in containers, especially Mid-Century hybrids like the orange 'Enchantment'. Plant lily bulbs as soon as you get them, in fall or spring, covering them with 5 to 6 inches of soil mix in deep pots. Use 1 bulb per 6-inch pot, several per larger container. Never let lilies dry out entirely, even when they are dormant. Grow in full sun to light shade. Different cultivars bloom successively from late spring through early fall.

Muscari armeniacum

Grape hyacinth

This charming small bulb bears dense, 8- to 12-inch spikes of berry-shaped blue flowers over a grasslike rosette of green leaves. The flowers are quite fragrant

and long lasting. There are other grape hyacinths of interest, some with feathery flowers and some with purple, violet, or white blooms. All bloom in early spring, just after the crocuses. Place in sun or light shade.

Narcissus

Daffodil, jonquil, narcissus

There is nearly an endless variety of narcissus: trumpet narcissus, short-cupped, double, and so on, with white or yellow petals and a central crown that ranges from the usual white or yellow to pink, orange, red, or green. All kinds do well in containers. Many are perfumed, some highly so. Plant many pots of them, including early to late varieties, to take full advantage of their potential. They do best in full sun to partial shade.

Ornithogalum nutans

Star-of-Bethlehem

The fragrant, nodding flowers of this plant are white inside and green with white stripes outside. They reach 8 to 12 inches in height over a low rosette

of tapering green leaves. *O. umbellatum*, also called star-of-Bethlehem, is similar but shorter (6 to 8 inches).

Scilla siberica

Siberian squill

This small, early-flowering bulb produces 6-inch stalks of nodding, deep blue flowers. It is particularly easy to grow in containers. 'Spring Beauty' is a choice cultivar in bright blue; 'Alba' has white flowers. Grow in sun or partial shade.

Tulipa

Tulip

Surely the queen of the spring bulbs, the tulip offers numerous forms and varieties in every shade of the rainbow—including green and deepest violet. Multiflowered tulips are especially showy in pots, as are dwarf varieties and those with colorful foliage, such as *T. greigii* and *T. praestans* 'Unicum'.

TENDER BULBS

Tender bulbs, for the most part, originate in Mediterranean climates around the world. They do not need cold treatment in order to bloom. Simply pot them up in the spring or fall, depending on when they are available, and water them, and they'll soon be in flower. Some of these flowers are evergreen, with leaves the year around; others die to the ground after blooming as hardy perennials do. The evergreen bulbs can be treated as perennial plants. Bulbs that die back after blooming can be removed from their pots, and stored in a cool spot for a few months before replanting.

Achimenes

Orchid pansy, mother's-tears

This fast-growing plant forms a dense, sometimes cascading mound of foliage and is covered for months on end with bright blue, pink, rose, purple, yellow, orange, or crimson flowers up to 3 inches wide. Start indoors in early spring with 3 to 5 tiny rhizomes per hanging basket.

Begonia tuberhybrida

Caladium bicolor

Plant 1 inch deep. Pinch once or twice early in the season to stimulate branching, then put it outside and let it flower the summer away. Never let it dry out during the growing season, or it will go dormant. The plant multiplies prolifically through numerous new rhizomes. It does best in partial shade.

Agapanthus

Lily-of-the-Nile, African lily

Lily-of-the-Nile is a striking container plant with long, dark green, straplike leaves. Its strong flower stalks bear globes of funnel-shaped blue, purple, or white flowers in midsummer. Larger forms, with flower stalks to 5 feet tall, are best grown in large tubs; dwarf hybrids, like 'Peter Pan' (blue, 2 feet tall) are well suited to ordinary pots. Plant the thick tuberous roots just below the surface of the soil. Most cultivars never go completely dormant, although you can cut back on watering and stop feeding when their growth slows. When fall frosts threaten, bring indoors and place in sun. Lily-of-the-Nile can be left outdoors permanently in areas where hard freezes are

rare. Divide only when the plant is completely root-bound, every 5 to 7 years.

Anemone coronaria

Florist's anemone

This plant is surprisingly hardy for a "tender" bulb—it can be grown in Zones 7 to 10—but it is best placed in this category because it doesn't require the cold dormant period that most hardy bulbs do. It produces 2- to 4-inch poppylike flowers in brilliant shades of white, lavender, mauve, pink, crimson, and scarlet, often with a contrasting black center and a lighter halo at the base of the petals. Flowers are solitary on 6- to 18-inch stems. It blooms heavily from late winter to midspring in warm climates and from late spring through the summer elsewhere, with some repetition in early fall. For best results, plant 1 to 2 inches deep outdoors in fall in warm-climate areas and start indoors in early spring in cool climates. Soak tubers overnight before planting. When

foliage dies back (in summer in the south, in fall in the north), dry them out thoroughly, storing them in a frost-free area. The best-known strains are 'St. Brigid' and 'De Caen', both in mixed colors. Anemone needs sun to partial shade. It makes an excellent cut flower.

Begonia tuberhybrida hybrids

Tuberous begonia

This is a highly popular plant, especially where summers are cool and humid. The flattened tuber produces thick, succulent stems and large, deep green leaves from which emerge exotic and spectacular flowers in the form of camellias, roses, or carnations, or in forms that are variously frilled and crested. The flowers are often enormous, to 6 inches in diameter, and come in red, pink, yellow, orange, or white, sometimes with a contrasting border. The smaller-blooming varieties—including Multifloras and the appropriately named 'Nonstop' varieties—are, however, more floriferous and also easier to grow, being less likely to suffer wind and rain damage than the

giant-flowered types. The latter also look good in hanging baskets, as do Pendulas, a series with trailing stems. Plant tubers indoors in late winter, barely covering them with soil. Keep them barely moist until they sprout. After all danger of frost is past, put them outdoors in filtered sun to moderate shade. When frost kills back the foliage in fall or when flowering slows, bring indoors and store dry until the following spring.

Caladium bicolor

Fancy-leaved caladium

There is probably no more colorful foliage plant available. The large, heart-shaped to lance-shaped leaves are extravagantly colored in white, pink, and red, often with contrasting veins or splatters of secondary colors. The flowers, which are insignificant, should be removed because producing them uses energy that would otherwise be used for better foliage. Plant tubers in late winter in a warm,

Canna × generalis

Cyclamen persicum

humid spot, barely covering them with soil mix, and keep well watered as new leaves appear. When nighttime temperatures are safely above 60° F, put outside in a partially to densely shaded spot. In fall, bring in and let dry. Store over winter as other dormant tender bulbs (see page 52). In warmer climates, start new tubers every 2 weeks for a continuous display throughout the year.

Canna × generalis
Canna

Large, tropical-looking green or bronze leaves, sometimes striped yellow, are only one of the charms of this popular container plant. The large spikes of often fiery flowers in scarlet, apricot, coral, pink, yellow, white, or bicolor are its main drawing card. For all its exotic appearance, the canna is an easy-to-grow plant. Start rhizomes indoors in spring, burying them 3 to 4 inches deep in large containers, and put them outside when the weather

has warmed. After blooming, cut plant back and bring inside for the winter. Store as recommended for tender bulbs (see page 52). The rhizomes can stay in the same container for several years before needing division. Dwarf cannas, from 18 inches to 3 feet, are the best choices for container culture.

Clivia miniata
Clivia

The evergreen, strap-shaped leaves of this plant are attractive in their own right. When it is in flower in late winter or early spring, the bright orange, funnel-shaped flowers are simply spectacular. Plant so the bulbous base is barely covered in mix. Place in a clay pot just 2 inches larger than the rootball, then let it grow until it threatens to burst its pot, as it blooms better when root-bound. In cool climates, put it outdoors in late spring in bright shade to full sun, then bring back indoors in fall to a brightly lit spot. It can remain outdoors the year around in frost-free climates. Water evenly from spring through summer, then, in fall, reduce water. If possible, buy

a mature specimen, as clivia grows slowly and can take 5 years or more to bloom from a small division.

Cyclamen persicum
Florist's cyclamen

This common gift plant can make a spectacular container specimen for spring bloom if properly treated. In late fall, pot into a container just larger than the tuber, leaving the top exposed. Place in a cool spot and keep the soil barely moist until sprouting begins. Move outdoors to semishade or shade as soon as possible in spring. Transfer to a cool, dry spot, such as under a roof overhang or a shady toolshed, when the foliage fades in summer. Butterfly-shaped flowers in white, pink, red, or purple, often with two or more shades on the same plant, appear in great numbers on individual stalks over silvery marbled, heart-shaped leaves. Cyclamen, which is deciduous, grows to 12 inches in height.

Dahlia pinnata hybrids
Dahlia

This extremely popular flowering plant offers thousands of named varieties of different forms, colors, and sizes. In general, they resemble double, semidouble, or single daisies, often bicolored, in all shades but true blue and green. Dwarf to medium-height varieties, growing to 3 feet high, are best for container culture. Plant tuberous roots 6 inches deep in large containers. Start indoors in late winter to extend the blooming season. Bring indoors in fall and store dry in a cool place. Divide regularly before potting up. See page 46 for information on annual types.

Freesia hybrids
Freesia

Highly scented, trumpet-shaped flowers in white, yellow, orange, pink, red, purple, or violet are borne in spikelike clusters on 18-inch stalks. The leaves are sword shaped. Start corms outdoors in fall for winter blooms in warm climates, and indoors in winter for spring blooms elsewhere. Plant 2 inches deep, 6 to

Freesia species

Ranunculus asiaticus

8 per 6-inch pot. Stagger plantings for continuous bloom. Keep cool and slightly moist throughout growing period, moving outdoors when all danger of frost is passed. Flowers may need staking. Allow pots to dry off when flowers fade and store dry in their pots until the following season.

Ixia

Corn lily

Red, pink, yellow, orange, or white flowers are borne on wiry 18- to 24-inch stems in late spring. Foliage is grasslike. Pot corms 2 inches deep, 6 per 6-inch pot, in fall. Keep cool and moist indoors in a sunny place, then set out in full sun when all danger of frost is past. In summer, allow corms to dry off and store dry in their pots until the following season. Containers can remain outdoors the year around where winters are cool, humid, and frost free and summers are hot and dry.

Ranunculus asiaticus

Florist's ranunculus

Spectacular, fully double, 3- to 5-inch flowers in white, red, pink, gold, orange, and bronze make the 12- to 18-inch ranunculus a favorite container plant. Soak claw-shaped tuberous roots in water overnight before planting 1 inch deep, 1 per 6-inch pot, with claws pointing down, in midwinter. Keep cool and moist, moving outside to a cool spot when all danger of frost is passed. Each tuberous root produces dozens of flowers until summer heat cuts off the display. Store dry over summer and fall, then repeat process in midwinter.

Sparaxis tricolor

Harlequin flower

Yellow, rose, red, orange, and purple flowers with a contrasting center up to 2 inches wide are produced on 18-inch stems over lance-shaped leaves. Pot corms 2 inches deep, 5 or 6 per

6-inch pot in fall. Keep cool and moist indoors in a sunny place, then set out in full sun when all danger of frost is past. In summer, allow corms to dry off and store dry in their pots until the following season. Containers can remain outdoors the year around in areas with cool winters and dry summers.

Zephyranthes

Zephyr lily, rain lily

This plant makes a spectacular container plant, blooming off and on throughout the year, indoors and out. The crocuslike flowers measure 2 to 4 inches across in white, pink, purple, red, or yellow and are borne on 12-inch stems over tufts of grassy foliage. Plant 10 to 12 bulbs per 6-inch pot, 2 inches deep. Keep soil moist until they bloom, then allow pot to dry out in a hot sunny spot for 10 weeks before watering again. This ability of the plants to flower rapidly, several times a year, after rains begin gives them the name *rain lily*. Leave outdoors during the frost-free season; bring in for the winter.

SHRUBS

Because shrubs are so useful in the garden, most garden centers carry a wide selection. You are likely to find almost any shrub that grows in your area in a local garden center. In the ground, shrubs are often seen as the "bones" of the garden. Serving as its permanent shapes, they define space and shape the garden "rooms." They also have this function in containers. A row of containerized shrubs can be used as a temporary barrier or screen, but they're more commonly used as accent plants. The size and mass of shrubs demands attention. Many flower, and all can be pruned to interesting and attractive shapes. Perhaps the most dramatic pruning is topiary, whereby shrubs are pruned into geometrical shapes or frequently whimsical sculptures.

Bougainvillea hybrid

Cycas revoluta

Abelia × *grandiflora*

Glossy abelia

Evergreen to semideciduous. A colorful combination of foliage and flowers, this shrub has gracefully arching branches and leaves that are coppery when new, then gradually turn glossy green. Flower clusters bloom white to pinkish white from early summer into fall. Prune selectively in late winter. For best color, place in full sun. Hardy to Zone 7.

Berberis thunbergii 'Atropurpurea'

Japanese barberry

Deciduous. The finely textured, colorful foliage of this shrub makes it a good portable barrier. Leaves are bronzy red in spring and summer, then turn yellow, orange, and red in fall. Red berries are revealed after leaves drop. It has a dense habit and arching, heavily thorned branches. It can be sheared, but is more attractive when pruned selectively. Grow in full sun. Hardy to Zone 4.

Variety 'Atropurpurea Nana' is dwarf.

Bougainvillea hybrids

Bougainvillea

Evergreen to semievergreen. A woody subtropical vine suitable for container culture, bougainvillea is often grown with great success as a hanging plant or bonsai subject. Among the hybrids are 'Raspberry Ice' with bright red flowers and variegated leaves, and 'Crimson Jewel', with crimson flowers. Transplant with great care, as the roots are fussy. Hang in a sunny, sheltered southern exposure. Take indoors during winter except in frost-free areas. Hardy to Zone 10.

Buxus microphylla koreana

Korean boxwood

Evergreen. Although well known as a small hedge or edging plant, this boxwood is most picturesque when trained into a formal shape and planted in a container. It stays low-growing (3 feet) and compact without severe pruning, and has tiny, bright green leaves. It grows well in sun or partial shade. Hardy to Zone 5.

B. microphylla japonica and its several varieties and *B. sempervirens,* including the dwarf variety 'Suffruticosa', are excellent container shrubs.

Camellia hybrids

Camellia

Evergreen. All members of this handsome genus grow well in tubs if they are given acid soil, partial shade, and protection from drying winds. There are a number of varieties, which bloom at different times from fall to late spring. In cold areas, a cool sunporch is ideal for them in winter.

Some small, sprawling varieties of *Camellia sasanqua* lend themselves beautifully to hanging planters. Among the best are 'Showa-No-Sakae' and 'Shishi Gashira'. Give them shelter from heavy rain. Hardy to Zone 9.

Chamaecyparis obtusa

Hinoki false cypress

Evergreen. Slow to outgrow its place and easy to keep below 6 feet, this tree can be trained to reveal its attractive irregular branching pattern. The dwarf Hinoki false cypress (*C. obtusa* 'Nana'), growing only 3 feet high, is round headed with deep green foliage on layered branches. The golden Hinoki false cypress (*C. obtusa* 'Aurea') has golden new foliage that gradually turns deep green. All Hinoki false cypresses make excellent bonsai specimens. They are unsatisfactory in hot-summer areas. Hardy to Zone 8 and below, depending on the cultivar.

Cotoneaster species

Cotoneaster

This genus offers many good container plants, including two that are outstanding as hanging basket plants: bearberry cotoneaster (*C. dammeri*) and creeping cotoneaster (*C. adpressus*). Creeping cotoneaster, a deciduous shrub, grows slowly to a height of 12 inches and bears pink flowers followed by bright red berries. Bearberry cotoneaster also provides a cascading display of white flowers and red berries. It has evergreen foliage (deciduous in exposed sites) and reaches a height of 12 inches. Grow cotoneaster in full sun or partial shade. Hardy to Zone 5.

Fuchsia hybrid

Hedera helix

Cycas revoluta

Sago palm

Evergreen. One of the most striking plants for containers, this relic of distant geologic ages has characteristics of both fern and palm. Very slow growing, it seldom exceeds 2 to 3 feet in height, even in old age. It prefers little water and fertilizer. Although it can take temperatures down to 20° F for short periods, it should be taken indoors in winter in all but the warmest climates.

Euonymus fortunei

Winter-creeper

Many varieties of this woody evergreen vine make hardy ground covers, and their wide-spreading habit works for hanging baskets as well. Keep wayward branches pruned when grown in hanging baskets. The dark green leaves of trailing winter-creeper (*Euonymus fortunei* var. *radicans*) are smaller than most. The purple-leaved winter-creeper variety 'Coloratus' drapes nicely, as will the green and white variegated form 'Variegatus'. Grow in full sun or partial shade. Euonymus is hardy to Zone 4.

Fuchsia hybrids

Fuchsia

Deciduous or evergreen. Selected varieties of fuchsias are at the top of the list for hanging-basket plants in the "fuchsia climates"—the cool coastal areas. In hot-summer regions, fuchsia enthusiasts must resort to mist-spraying to give the plant the climate it needs. Fuchsias will survive a light frost, although leaves and young growth will be injured. In hard-frost areas, treat as an annual, take cuttings for next spring, or bring the entire plant indoors. Spring is the time for pruning. Cut back approximately the same amount of growth made the previous summer or remove frost-injured wood. Fuchsias bloom early and continue through summer to frost. Hang baskets in a location protected from wind and in a partially shaded exposure. In cold-winter areas fuchsias can be overwintered by cutting them back and packing their containers in plastic trash cans of moist sawdust or vermiculite, stored at about 40° to 50° F.

Hedera helix varieties

English ivy

Evergreen. In addition to the regular garden form of this classic woody-stemmed ground and wall cover, with its 2- to 4-inch leaves, there are many attractive varieties with miniature leaves—all ideal for hanging baskets. Some have variegated or ruffled leaves. Complementing their beauty and ease of cultivation is the advantage of their year-round uniform appearance. If you can't find them at a nursery or garden center, try houseplant stores and florists. Some favorites are 'Fluffy Ruffles', 'Gold Dust', 'Hahn's', 'Needlepoint', 'Pixie', and 'Silver King'. Many hardy to Zone 3 or 4.

Hibiscus rosa-sinensis

Chinese hibiscus

Evergreen. Yielding lavish summer color, this plant sports glossy leaves and large (4- to 8-inch), showy, single or double flowers in shades of pink, red, yellow, and white. Choose among many varieties for flower color and plant habit. Warm weather and sun promote the best bloom; Chinese hibiscus needs afternoon shade in the hottest areas. Since it is cold sensitive (taking temperatures to 20° F for short periods with overhead protection), bring it indoors in cold-winter areas.

Hibiscus syriacus

Shrub-althea, rose-of-Sharon

Deciduous. This widely used member of the genus *Hibiscus* blooms in an array of single or double flowers (2½ to 3 inches) in pink, red, purple, or violet in summer. Foliage is bright green, unevenly toothed, and sometimes lobed. Erect and compact when young, it requires pruning to shape when older. In winter, partially prune last year's growth for larger flowers the following summer. It does well in partial shade or fall sun. Hardy to Zone 5.

Hydrangea macrophylla

Lantana camara

Hydrangea macrophylla

Hydrangea

Deciduous. This shrub creates a soft feeling that seems to invite relaxation. Large clusters of white, pink, red, or blue flowers hide the foliage in summer and fall. Flower color is easily manipulated by soil pH, turning blue in acid soil and deepest red in alkaline. Large leaves (8 inches) are glossy and toothed. It has an even, round habit. Prune to desired size. Grow in full sun in cool-summer areas; give it afternoon shade in hot-summer areas. Hardy to Zone 5.

Ilex species

Holly

Evergreen. The glossy green foliage and bright red berries are a classic reminder of the holiday season. For large, long-lasting berries on a slow-growing compact plant, try Chinese holly (*Ilex cornuta* 'Burfordii'). Hardy to Zone 7. The many forms of English holly (*I. aquifolium*) are just as good in containers, although they are less tolerant of dry heat.

Dwarf forms of yaupon holly (*I. vomitoria*), with small spineless leaves, make excellent container shrubs. All are hardy to Zone 8.

Lagerstroemia indica

Crape myrtle

Deciduous. Usually thought of as a tree, crape myrtle is also grown as a small hanging-basket shrub. The 'Dixie' series makes cascading 24-inch mounds and includes 10 different flower colors. 'Bayou Marie' is a dazzling bicolor. 'Bourbon Street' is watermelon red. Hardy to Zone 8.

Lantana species

Lantana

Evergreen or deciduous. In mild-winter areas this trailing shrub can add year-round color to the container garden. Plants are easily damaged by light frosts, but unless the soil freezes, they'll often survive to give full bloom the following year—just trim out deadwood to maintain a neat appearance. Put in a warm, full-sun spot, and don't overwater or overfertilize. Take indoors in cold-winter areas. Some of the more colorful

cultivars are 'Carnival' (crimson, lavender, yellow, and pink), 'Confetti' (pink, yellow, and purple), and 'Gold Mound' (yellow-orange). Trailing forms make excellent hanging basket plants. Particularly good is the 'Spreading' series. Hardy to Zone 10.

Lavandula angustifolia

English lavender

Evergreen. Highly valued for its fragrance, this small (12- to 48-inch) shrub is a pleasant addition to any patio. Strongly fragrant lavender to purple flowers are borne on long (18- to 24-inch) spikes in midsummer. Its gray foliage is also aromatic. Prune after flowering to maintain compactness. Other species of lavender and varieties of English lavender are occasionally available. Hardy in all areas to Zone 4.

Nandina domestica

Heavenly-bamboo

Evergreen. A light, airy shrub with an oriental, bamboolike feel, it has many slender, unbranched stems bearing softly textured leaves divided into leaflets. Pinkish bronze foliage gradually turns green, then picks up a purple or bronze tinge in fall, and becomes scarlet in the winter sun. Although it grows 6 to 8 feet, it is easily controlled. Dwarf varieties are available. Heavenly-bamboo produces bright red berries in fall on the female plants if one male plant is nearby. Hardy to Zone 7.

Pinus mugo

Mugo pine

Dwarf forms of this pine, such as 'Compacta', 'Gnom' or 'Slavinii', remain tiny, compact shrubs. With a little pruning, a specimen makes a striking bonsai. Mugo pine is an ideal candidate for container growth. If you find that yours is getting higher than you want it, pinch new, soft green shoots (candles) to 1 inch in spring. Foliage is attractively dense. Hardy to Zone 3.

Pinus mugo

Chamaedorea elegans

Rhododendron species and hybrids

Rhododendron and azalea

Some deciduous, most evergreen. These magnificent plants adapt beautifully to container culture as long as they have ample containers, acid soil, generous water, fast drainage, protection from burning sun in hot climates, and protection from extreme cold. Small types of rhododendrons are easiest for container culture. All evergreen azaleas adapt. For hanging baskets, *Azalea macrantha* 'Gumpo' (white) and 'Gumpo Pink', both spreading and slightly pendulous, are excellent choices for spring color. The more tender azaleas and rhododendrons need indoor protection in winter in most climates, although a few deciduous azaleas are hardy to below 0° F if their containers are insulated.

TREES

Like shrubs, trees command attention in the garden for their size if for no other reason. Placing a tree in a container seems to call attention to its shape. The effect is a little like framing a picture; an attractive tree in a container will draw more attention and reap more comments than would the same tree if it were growing in the ground. If your favorite tree is missing from this list, remember that the list is limited to trees that in most cases do not require a great deal of effort to keep pruned and shaped for container display.

Acer palmatum

Japanese maple

Deciduous. The Japanese maple in its various forms is commonly used in cool-summer gardens. It grows so slowly that it can be held in a tub for years as a small, dainty containerized tree. Many grafted garden forms are smaller than the seedlings. Of these, you might consider 'Burgundy Lace', whose deeply cut, serrated burgundy leaves on green stems have a soft lacy effect. 'Dissectum', which is easily

trained, has a low, weeping habit. Finely cut, fernlike green leaves are scarlet in fall. Most cultivars are hardy to Zone 4.

Cercis canadensis

Eastern redbud

Deciduous. For an early-spring flower show, the redbud will satisfy even the most demanding observer. Small, pealike clusters of pink, purple, or white flowers completely cover the leafless branches. Heart-shaped leaves provide summer shade ideal for patios and turn yellow in fall. Showy seed pods are revealed in late fall after the leaves drop; they remain on the tree into winter. Of the many cultivars, 'Forest Pansy' is of interest, with pinkish purple flowers and foliage on red stems. 'Alba' is a profusely flowering variety. Hardy to Zone 4.

Palms

Several palms lend themselves to container culture. Palms have a fibrous root system that adapts well to containers, but the larger ones don't dwarf as readily as other woody plants, and they outgrow their containers too rapidly. For this reason, the choice is limited to the smaller palms.

Chamaedorea elegans

Parlor palm

Evergreen. This palm has typical fish-skeleton-like leaf bases that sheath the single trunk, merging in a cluster at the top.

Several other palms lend themselves equally well to container culture. The paradise palm (*Howea forsteriana*) has similar leaves on a clean, interestingly scarred, 9-foot stem. The pygmy date palm (*Phoenix roebelenii*) grows slowly to 6 feet. Its airy leaves emerge from the top of the slender stem. The lady palm (*Rhapis excelsa*), an old favorite in containers, grows 6 to 12 feet tall. Its many stalks bear oriental-fanlike foliage at the tips, making for a bushy effect resembling bamboo.

Ginkgo biloba

Lagerstroemia indica

These palms are strictly tropical plants, and will not take freezing. But some others will. For example, the popular Mediterranean fan palm (*Chamaerops humilis*) withstands temperatures in the teens or lower for short periods, if the container is insulated.

Cornus florida

Flowering dogwood

Deciduous. Flowering dogwoods signal the beginning of spring with a spectacular show, and deserve to be featured in your landscape. Flowers appear before foliage in shades of red, pink, rose, or white. Foliage turns bright red in fall, highlighted by red berries. Its slow growth when young (to 10 to 15 feet) makes it a good container candidate. It is a perfect companion for the eastern redbud (*Cercis canadensis*). Hardy to Zone 4.

Crataegus phaenopyrum

Washington thorn

Deciduous. Put this tree in a container on your patio, and you will be rewarded with color through spring, summer, and fall. White flowers blooin profusely in spring to early summer. Attractive clusters of red berries appear in late summer through winter. Lobed leaves are brilliant orange-red in fall. It has a dense, graceful, low-branching habit, and 1- to 3-inch thorns. Hardy to Zone 4.

Ginkgo biloba

Ginkgo, maidenhair tree

Deciduous. This large tree can be held to container size for years. Its light green, fan-shaped leaves dance in the wind, providing a summer-long attraction whether moving or still. In the fall, the leaves turn a rich, bright yellow. The fact that this survivor of prehistoric times is sometimes called a living fossil and is considered the oldest tree on earth hints at its hardiness and versatility. Give it the toughest spot in the garden and watch it thrive. To be sure to get a male tree (fruits of the

females are messy and have an unpleasant smell), choose named cultivars such as 'Autumn Gold', 'Lakeview', or 'Sentry'. Hardy to Zone 3.

Lagerstroemia indica

Crape myrtle

Deciduous. In summer, when flowering trees are hard to find, crape myrtle comes across in style. Crinkled, crapelike flowers in shades of white, pink, rose, or lavender bloom over a long period. The light green leaves turn orange-red in fall. The mottled tan bark and branching pattern are more apparent during the leafless winter months and add a note of interest to a possibly bland landscape. The root system is sufficiently hardy to encourage use at the low-temperature limits of its range.

A group of crape myrtles called Indian Tribe has superior hardiness, performance, and mildew resistance. Named cultivars include red-flowering 'Cherokee', purple-flowering

'Catawba', pink-flowering 'Potomac' and 'Seminole', and light lavender 'Powhatan'. The tree is generally hardy to Zone 6, but check the tolerance of individual cultivars.

Malus species

Flowering crab apple

Deciduous. Considering the many varieties of crab apple available, there is surely one that will fit your garden scheme. Valued for their delicate, profuse spring flowers in shades of white, pink, and red, crab apples come in a wide range of habits and foliage colors as well. The tree shape ranges from weeping to columnar.

Leaf color is primarily green, but some leaves retain a reddish bronze color for the entire season. Fruits are attractive from late summer to early winter. Most crab apples are hardy to at least Zone 4.

When selecting a variety of crab apple, be sure to watch for disease resistance and hardiness of individual cultivars. The following crab apples suitable for containers have acceptable disease resistance.

Picea glauca 'Conica'

Pinus thunbergii

'Callaway'. Pink buds open to large white flowers (1 to 1½ inches). Reddish maroon ¾- to 1¼-inch fruits. Round-headed form. One of the best choices for warmer climates.

Japanese flowering crab apple (*M. floribunda*). Mound-like and horizontally branching. Flowers are pink, fading to white. Fruits are yellow-red, ⅜ inch.

'Molten Lava'. Wide spreading with weeping habit. Attractive yellow bark. Flowers are deep red in bud, opening white. Fruits are red-orange, ⅜ inch, lasting until December.

Parkman crab apple (*M. halliana* 'Parkmanii'). Gracefully arching purple branches. Flowers are large, double, and rose. Fruits are dull red, ¼ inch.

Sargent crab apple (*M. sargentii*). Lowest and broadest of the crab apples (8 to 10 feet high and 12 feet wide). Flowers are white. Fruits are small, red, in clusters.

Picea glauca 'Conica'

Dwarf Alberta spruce

Evergreen. You can probably look over the top of even an old specimen of this dwarf conifer, which grows only about an inch per year. Fine textured, dense, and perfectly conical, it is a favorite as a living Christmas tree. (If you take it indoors for Christmas, give it light, keep it away from dry heat, and return it to its outdoor spot in 10 days or sooner.) Protect from unusually hot sun and drying winds. Hose it down occasionally in hot weather. Hardy to Zone 3.

Pinus thunbergii

Japanese black pine

Evergreen. A favorite for bonsai training, it is equally valuable as a tub specimen. It grows slowly and may take 3 to 4 years to reach 4 feet. In a large container, given time, it becomes a small tree, though is easily shaped and kept at desired size. Hardy to Zone 4.

Podocarpus macrophyllus

Yew pine

Evergreen. This slow-growing tree (not a true pine) is valuable indoors and out, and is good in containers. Leaves are 4 inches long and narrow. The yellowish green new foliage contrasts nicely with the older, dark green leaves, giving a fernlike effect. A tender native of Japan, it is hardy to Zone 8. It can be brought indoors for the winter in cold climates.

Prunus species

Flowering plums

Deciduous. When you think about the flowering plums, you have to consider more than the spring flowers alone; their purple foliage is a strong element in any garden.

Prunus cerasifera 'Atropurpurea' and its related forms— 'Thundercloud', 'Newport', 'Vesuvius'—are widely available. Hardy to Zone 4.

P. × *blireana* is a popular, nearly fruitless tree. It has reddish bronze foliage and bears pink double flowers, in contrast to the pink single clusters of the 'Atropurpurea' forms. *P. blireana* also has a lighter, more graceful form than the 'Atropurpurea' and its variations. Hardy to Zone 4.

Prunus caroliniana

Carolina cherry-laurel

Evergreen. No bright, unusual colors here—just a dense, glossy tree that offers a luxurious touch of green. Small white flowers appear in late winter or early spring, with black berries following. Whether single or multiple trunked, it is easily trained into formal shapes. Two cultivars ideal for containers are 'Bright 'n Tight' and 'Compacta'. Hardy to Zone 7.

Wisteria species

Dwarf marsh seedless grapefruit

Pyrus kawakamii

Evergreen pear

Evergreen. Left untouched, it becomes a sprawling shrub. Tied to a trellis or wire, it can easily be trained as an espalier. Staked, it makes a handsome single-trunked tree. The glossy green foliage is a year-round attraction. Fragrant white flowers are abundant in late winter or early spring. It is fast growing. Heavy pruning reduces flowering. It may not survive extreme cold. Hardy to Zone 9.

Wisteria species

Wisteria

Deciduous. This vigorous woody vine can be trained as a small, single-trunked tree with an umbrellalike top. The "tree" produces the same long, lovely clusters of blossoms that have earned this long-lived woody plant the description "queen of the vines."

Flowers are borne in spring in shades of white, pink, blue, or lavender. Their fragrance is evocative of warm spring evenings. Leaves are 12 to 18 inches long and are divided into leaflets. Hardy to Zone 4.

CITRUS TREES

All types of citrus are old favorites for container gardening. They are attractive in leaf and shape, and bear intensely fragrant flowers followed by delicious and elegant fruit. They also have a long bloom and fruit period; some carry flowers and fruit for most of the growing season. In addition to the citruses listed below, grapefruit, limequat, tangelo, citron, tangerine, and Nagami kumquat are available in dwarfed varieties.

Calamondin

This naturally dwarf citrus produces abundant 1- to 2-inch, orangelike fruits every month of the year. Since they are too bitter to eat, leave them on the tree to brighten the surroundings, or use them to make marmalade.

Dwarf 'Washington Navel' Orange

This popular juice orange bears in areas too cool for successful cultivation of other oranges. Harvest from winter into spring.

Fruit peels easily. Maximum height of tree is 8 feet.

'Meyer' Lemon

This dwarf is a relatively old variety, bearing flowers that range in color from lavender to white, followed by bright yellow lemons with thin skin and sweet flavor.

'Otaheite' Orange

This miniature version of the sweet orange produces 1- to 2-inch fruits that taste more like a lime than an orange. They can remain on the tree for as long as 2 years.

Persian Lime

For full-sized fruit, this is the dwarf lime to grow. The fruit is bright chartreuse-green, and the plant is easily kept small for an indefinite period.

'Ponderosa' Lemon

Probably the most spectacular of the dwarf citruses, this one has glossy green leaves, short spines, and giant lemons that weigh from 1 to 3 pounds. Each

one takes about 6 months to mature, but this plant has fruit at varying stages of maturity the year around. As fruits approach maturity, prop branches with stakes.

DECIDUOUS FRUIT TREES

Growing certain deciduous fruits in containers, including those grafted onto dwarfing rootstocks, is discussed in the previous chapter on page 54. Almost any fruit is available in this form. You can select your favorite variety of apple or pear and order it grafted to dwarfing rootstock. The most compact, however, are the genetic (true) dwarf varieties developed especially for container culture. These are not dwarfed by grafting, but are natural dwarf trees. Full-size fruit is borne heavily—sometimes so heavily that developing fruit requires thinning. Most trees grow slowly to no more than 5 to 8 feet. Genetic dwarfs are described here.

Dwarf nectarine

Dwarf peach

'Apple Babe' Apple

This tiny genetic dwarf apple reaches only 4 feet tall and 3 feet wide. The yellow and red fruit is large and very tasty. Plant with 'Garden Delicious' or another containerized apple for pollination.

Colonnade Apples

These narrowly upright apple trees are a new concept in apple growing. They produce flowers and fruits on short spurs originating directly from the trunk, without the spreading branches so typical of other apple trees. The result is a tree only 2 feet wide and 8 feet tall. Yet given the small space it occupies, it is every bit as productive as a regular dwarf apple tree. Among other cultivars, look for 'Emerald-Spire' (green apples with a golden blush), 'ScarletSpire' (red over green), Crimson-Spire (red with white flesh), and 'UltraSpire' (red with a yellow-green blush). All require a pollinator—a good reason for buying a second tree. Hardy in Zones 4 to 8.

'Garden Delicious' Apple

Derived from the popular 'Golden Delicious', this fruit can be eaten fresh or used for cooking. To encourage early growth, the first year remove all fruit before it develops, and the second year remove most. Remove suckers from rootstock. This is the most widely available dwarf apple. Self-fertile.

'Garden Annie' Apricot

This semifreestone takes 3 years to reach harvesting size. Among the larger genetic dwarf trees, it needs occasional pruning to keep its center open to air and light. Self-fertile.

'Garden Bing' Cherry

Slow growing to about 6 feet, the tree has a 4-foot spread. Occasional branches revert to standard size and should be removed. Self-fertile.

'North Star Sour' Cherry

This tangy cooking cherry bears large fruit in late June on a tree that reaches 8 feet. Self-fertile.

'Nectar Babe' Nectarine

Comparable in fruit quality, and in beauty of blooms and fruit, to 'Honey Babe' peach, it bears prolifically. It also needs occasional pruning to keep its center open. It is self-fertile but bears more heavily if a 'Honey Babe' peach is close by.

'Honey Babe' Peach

Only 4 to 6 feet tall at maturity, this tree has especially close-noded stems, so it bears heavily. Freestone fruit is early ripening, and quality is excellent. It is exceptionally beautiful in bloom and in fruit. Prune to keep center open. Self-fertile.

SMALL FRUITS

Brambles and grapes are awkward sizes for container culture but, with the proper handling, perform satisfactorily. Blueberries and strawberries are excellent container plants. Berries and grapes need specific pruning to bear well; prune them and remove old canes as if the plants were in the ground.

Blackberries

Although blackberries in containers can easily be trained up trellises in the traditional manner, it is much simpler to let them grow as nature intended: as trailers. For ease of harvest, choose thornless varieties, such as 'Chester' and 'Navaho Thornless'. Prune out branches that have already borne fruit to leave room for new growth. Give full sun to partial shade. Self-fertile. Zones 6 to 7. Boysenberries, loganberries, and tayberries are similar.

Blueberries (highbush)

Blueberries make attractive shrubs in their own right, with tall, vigorous growth, attractive pinkish to white bell-shaped

Blueberries

Strawberries

flowers, beautiful fall color, and thick clusters of blue to black berries. Use an acid soil mix, or make one with half peat moss and half commercial potting mix. Place in full sun or partial shade. Don't hesitate to prune these tall growers to the height you prefer. Different varieties ripen at different times, so choose several for a long harvest season. Two popular varieties are 'Bluecrop' (very early) and 'Elliot' (late). Zones 4 to 7.

Blueberries (lowbush)

As their name suggests, these blueberries are low growing, reaching only 12 to 18 inches high, and make good ground covers around tall-growing container trees and shrubs. They are evergreen and attractive in all seasons, taking on a bright red coloration in fall. Use an acid soil mix (see above). Most are self-sterile, so plant at least two cultivars. 'Northsky' (mid-season) and 'North Country' (early) are popular choices. Zones 2 to 6.

Grapes

Choose table grapes for container culture. Grapes are quite productive when their roots are restricted by a container. Use one 10-gallon pot per plant. Prune heavily for maximum production. Supply a trellis or arbor on which the grapes can climb. Self-fertile. Hardiness and productivity of grape cultivars are closely linked to regional climatic conditions: check with local garden centers for varieties well adapted to your climate.

Raspberries

Invasive in the garden, the rampantly growing raspberry is automatically controlled in containers. The result is a delicately arching plant with attractive reddish stems, pretty white, roselike blooms, and pleasing—and delicious—red, purple, black, or yellow fruits. Prune old canes in the fall. The so-called ever-bearing raspberries (actually, they produce two crops: one in July, one in September)

are the best choices for container culture. 'Summit' and 'Heritage' are two choice red everbearing varieties. Self-fertile. Zones 3 to 7.

Strawberries

Among the most attractive of all the small fruits, strawberries are naturals for container culture. You can grow them in hanging baskets, in clay and wood strawberry barrels, in 5-gallon plastic pails, in planter boxes, and along walls. For maximum production, the container should be large enough to nourish a root system at least 8 inches wide and 8 inches deep. Restricting the root system by planting in an overly small container reduces production; reducing any part of the root system affects the entire plant. All strawberry varieties do well in containers. Select varieties recommended by a local garden center or cooperative extension office.

VEGETABLES

Most gardeners don't realize the volume of produce that can be produced in a small space—even as small as a container. Especially if you have limited ground in which to plant vegetables, containers can yield a wealth of fresh produce. Although some vegetables take special arrangements, almost all can be grown in containers. As you peruse the seed racks or catalog pages, look for dwarf varieties. Some varieties have been developed just for containers. These are often compact and stocky.

All vegetables grow better and taste better if grown rapidly, with full sun and plenty of water and fertilizer. The best way to be sure their growth isn't checked is to water with a drip irrigation system controlled by a timer. This allows them to be watered daily or even twice a day if necessary. Check frequently to be sure each plant is getting enough water. Vegetables use water in direct proportion to their size; as they grow, they need to be watered more frequently. Fertilize them either with an attachment to the drip system that meters small

'Savoy Ace' cabbage

'Pot Luck' cucumber

amounts of liquid fertilizer into each irrigation, or with slow-release fertilizers in the potting mix. Either method ensures a steady supply of nutrients.

Beans

Planting Season Late spring, early summer

Light Full sun

Sowing Depth ½ to 1 inch

Spacing Bush beans: 2 to 3 inches; pole beans: 4 to 6 inches

Container 10 to 12 inches deep

Days to Maturity Bush beans: 45 to 65; pole beans: 60 to 70

Harvest Before seeds harden inside pod

Comments For a continuous crop of bush beans, sow every 2 weeks until midsummer. Pole beans will produce all season if harvested regularly.

Beets

Planting Season Early spring, fall

Light Tolerates partial shade

Sowing Depth ½ inch

Spacing 2 to 3 inches apart

Container At least 8 inches deep

Days to Maturity 55 to 65

Harvest When 1 to 2 inches in diameter

Comments Use thinnings as salad greens.

Broccoli

Planting Season Early summer

Light Full sun

Sowing Depth 1½ to 2 inches

Spacing 15 inches apart

Container At least 8 inches deep

Days to Maturity 60 to 80 from transplants

Harvest Before buds open

Comments Bears a second crop of side shoots when the main stalks are harvested.

Cabbage

Planting Season Needs cool weather to mature. Planting times differ among varieties.

Light Full sun

Sowing Depth ½ inch

Spacing 12 to 24 inches apart

Days to Maturity 65 to 95 from transplants

Container At least 10 inches deep

Harvest After heads form

Comments Use thinnings for salads.

Carrots

Planting Season Spring, early summer, fall

Light Tolerates partial shade

Sowing Depth ¼ inch

Spacing 1½ to 3 inches apart in a row. Thin early to avoid tangled roots.

Days to Maturity 60 to 80

Container At least 12 inches deep. Must have loose, deep soil.

Harvest For small carrots, harvest when ½ to 1 inch in diameter.

Comments Sow every 2 weeks until mid-June for continuous harvest. Choose short-rooted varieties.

Corn

Planting Season Summer; requires heat.

Light Full sun

Sowing Depth 2 inches

Spacing Grow in clusters of 4, planted about 6 inches apart, for pollination.

Container At least 8 inches deep

Days to Maturity 60 to 90

Harvest As soon as ears develop

Comments Don't stint on container size. Water and fertilize generously. Choose moderately short varieties.

Cucumbers

Planting Season Warm summer

Light Full sunlight

Sowing Depth 1 inch

Spacing 12 to 16 inches apart

Container At least 12 inches deep

Days to Maturity 55 to 65

Harvest Before hard seeds form

Comments A great many varieties. Train strong vining types on a trellis. One plant produces 20 to 30 fruits. Bush types, designed for containers, produce vines only 18 to 24 inches long.

Romaine lettuce

'Sweet Banana' pepper

Eggplant

Planting Season   Warm summer

Light   Full sun

Sowing Depth   ¼ to ½ inch

Spacing   One plant per container

Container   4- to 5-gallon size

Days to Maturity   75 to 95 from transplants

Harvest   At any stage from one-third to two-thirds of the mature size. Good fruit has high gloss.

Comments   Choose early varieties in short-season areas. Standard varieties require high heat and a long growing season. In containers, the varieties with medium to small fruits carried high on the plant are more interesting than the low-growing, heavy-fruited varieties.

Lettuce

Planting Season   Early spring, fall

Light   Tolerates partial shade

Sowing Depth   ¼ to ½ inch

Spacing   Leaf lettuce: 4 to 6 inches apart; head lettuce: up to 10 inches apart

Container   Head lettuce: at least 8 inches deep; leaf lettuce: any container

Days to Maturity   Head lettuce: 45 to 60; leaf lettuce: 60 to 90

Harvest   Leaf lettuce can be harvested as it grows, leaf by leaf.

Comments   High temperatures and long days cause lettuce to flower (bolt). For all but early-spring and fall plantings, choose varieties that are slow to bolt.

Melons (including cantaloupe)

Planting Season   Summer

Light   Full sun

Sowing Depth   1 inch

Spacing   One plant per container

Container   5-gallon container

Days to Maturity   80 to 100

Harvest   When melons are fragrant

Comments   Choose bush-type hybrids.

Onions

Planting Season   Early spring and September.

Light   Green onions grow in partial shade; mature bulbs need full sun.

Sowing Depth   Sets: 1 to 2 inches; seeds: ½ inch

Spacing   2 inches apart

Container   Minimum 6 inches deep

Days to Maturity   Green onions: 50 to 60 from sets; mature onions: 95 to 120 from sets, 100 to 165 from seeds

Harvest   When 8 to 10 inches tall for green onions; when leaves fall over for storing onions

Comments   Leave one green onion every 4 inches or so to form a bulb, usable for cooking after they dry out. In spring, plant short-day varieties such as 'Excel' in southern U.S., long-day varieties such as 'Yellow Globe Danvers' in northern areas. In fall, plant short-day varieties.

Peas

Planting Season   Very early spring to early summer

Light   Sun in cool climates; partial shade in hot climates

Sowing Depth   2 inches

Spacing   2 to 3 inches apart

Container   At least 12 inches deep

Days to Maturity   65 to 85

Harvest   Edible pod peas: while pods are still flat; green peas: when pods are well filled, but peas not yet hard

Comments   Plant successive crops every 2 weeks until mid-June.

Peppers

Planting Season   Warm summer

Light   Full sun

Sowing Depth   ¼ inch

Spacing   14 to 18 inches apart

Container   One plant per 2- to 4-gallon container

Days to Maturity   60 to 80 from transplants

Harvest   When 2 to 3 inches in diameter for green bell peppers; after they color for other types

Potatoes

Tomatoes

Comments Almost any variety, hot or sweet, is worth displaying on patio or deck for its ornamental value—shiny green leaves, small white flowers, and fruits in many shapes and colors (green, yellow, and red).

Potatoes

Planting Season Late spring and early summer

Light Full sun

Sowing Depth 4 inches

Spacing 2 eyes per container

Container 5 gallons or larger

Days to Maturity 90 to 105

Harvest When tops die down

Comments Plant eyes three-fourths of the way down in container, adding mulch as potatoes grow, so you pick rather than dig them.

Radishes

Planting Season Early spring, fall

Light Full sun to light shade

Sowing Depth ½ inch

Spacing Thin to 1 inch apart

Days to Maturity 20 to 50

Container Any size

Harvest As soon as roots begin to swell

Comments All varieties do well in containers.

Spinach

Planting Season Early spring, fall

Light Full sun to light shade

Sowing Depth ½ inch

Spacing 5 inches

Container Any size

Days to Maturity 50 to 60

Harvest Before plants flower

Comments All varieties are excellent for containers.

Squash (summer)
(see Zucchini)

Swiss Chard

Planting Season Spring, summer, fall

Light Tolerates partial shade

Sowing Depth 1 inch

Spacing 4 to 5 inches

Container 6 to 8 inches deep

Days to Maturity 55 to 65

Harvest When leaves are 3 inches or more in length

Comments Only one planting is needed. Outer leaves may be harvested without injury to the plant. Swiss chard is a great "cut and come again" plant, and a good leafy vegetable for summer, when spinach, lettuce, and kale are out of season.

Tomatoes

Planting Season Start indoors in late spring; transport outdoors when night temperatures are above 60° F.

Light Full sun at least 6 hours a day

Sowing Depth ½ inch

Spacing 18 to 24 inches

Container 4- to 5-gallon container for strong, large-fruited varieties

Days to Maturity 55 to 90 from transplants

Harvest When fruits are fully colored

Comments There are hundreds of varieties. Check with nursery staff or a county extension agent for varieties especially adapted to your area. A number of varieties for container culture are available. If you are using garden soil or compost in your soil mix, you should favor disease-resistant varieties. Resistance is indicated by the initials *V* (verticillium), *F* (fusarium), and *N* (nematode). Using a sterilized soil mix of peat moss and vermiculite or perlite will help to avoid soil-borne diseases.

Zucchini

Planting Season When temperatures warm up

Light Best in full sun

Sowing Depth 1 inch

Spacing One plant per 5-gallon container

Container Larger than 12 inches in diameter, at least 24 inches deep

Days to Maturity 50 to 60

Harvest When 1½ to 2 inches in diameter

Comments One plant will produce 6 or more fruits per week. Use compact varieties.

Climate Zone Map

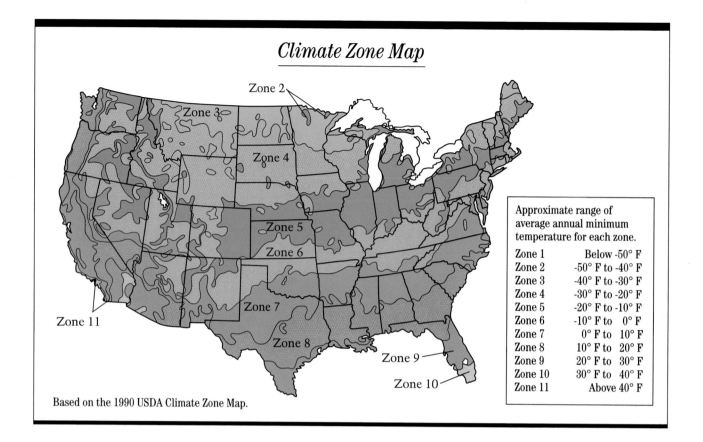

Approximate range of average annual minimum temperature for each zone.

Zone 1	Below -50° F
Zone 2	-50° F to -40° F
Zone 3	-40° F to -30° F
Zone 4	-30° F to -20° F
Zone 5	-20° F to -10° F
Zone 6	-10° F to 0° F
Zone 7	0° F to 10° F
Zone 8	10° F to 20° F
Zone 9	20° F to 30° F
Zone 10	30° F to 40° F
Zone 11	Above 40° F

Based on the 1990 USDA Climate Zone Map.

U.S. Measure and Metric Measure Conversion Chart

	Symbol	When you know:	Multiply by:	To find:	Rounded Measures for Quick Reference		
Mass	oz	ounces	28.35	grams	1 oz		= 30 g
(weight)	lb	pounds	0.45	kilograms	4 oz		= 115 g
	g	grams	0.035	ounces	8 oz		= 225 g
	kg	kilograms	2.2	pounds	16 oz	= 1 lb	= 450 g
					32 oz	= 2 lb	= 900 g
					36 oz	= 2¼ lb	= 1000 g (1 kg)
Volume	pt	pints	0.47	liters	1 c	= 8 oz	= 250 ml
	qt	quarts	0.95	liters	2 c (1 pt)	= 16 oz	= 500 ml
	gal	gallons	3.785	liters	4 c (1 qt)	= 32 oz	= 1 liter
	ml	milliliters	0.034	fluid ounces	4 qt (1 gal)	= 128 oz	= 3¾ liter
Length	in.	inches	2.54	centimeters	⅜ in.	= 1.0 cm	
	ft	feet	30.48	centimeters	1 in.	= 2.5 cm	
	yd	yards	0.9144	meters	2 in.	= 5.0 cm	
	mi	miles	1.609	kilometers	2½ in.	= 6.5 cm	
	km	kilometers	0.621	miles	12 in. (1 ft)	= 30 cm	
	m	meters	1.094	yards	1 yd	= 90 cm	
	cm	centimeters	0.39	inches	100 ft	= 30 m	
					1 mi	= 1.6 km	
Temperature	° F	Fahrenheit	⅝ (after subtracting 32)	Celsius	32° F	= 0° C	
	° C	Celsius	⅞ (then add 32)	Fahrenheit	212° F	= 100° C	
Area	in.²	square inches	6.452	square centimeters	1 in.²	= 6.5 cm²	
	ft²	square feet	929.0	square centimeters	1 ft²	= 930 cm²	
	yd²	square yards	8361.0	square centimeters	1 yd²	= 8360 cm²	
	a.	acres	0.4047	hectares	1 a.	= 4050 m²	

Formulas for Exact Measures